Many Beaucoup Magics

Tom Garvey

TOM GARVEY

ISBN-13: 978-1514228159

ISBN-10: 1514228157

Cover art by Brian Groth artwithanedge@yahoo.com

Back cover photo of Tom and Mozie by Len Lear courtesy of *Chestnut Hill Local*.

Technical assistance by Lois Hoffman, The Happy Self-Publisher
www.happyselfpublisher.com

Many Beaucoup Magics is dedicated to ALL the Mothers who suffered the loss of their children in the many wars in Vietnam. In any war, Mothers are the ultimate victims.

Table of Contents

"All that we see or seem

Is but a dream within a dream"

Edgar Allen Poe, Sergeant Major, United States Army

God Strike Me Dead

When Johnny McManus was a little boy, he thought World War II lasted forever. Grownups just couldn't let go of it. Every man he knew had been in the war, except his dad.

John's father, Jim, had a difficult childhood. He grew up on the waterfront without a father. A tough kid, a hard one, Jimmy McManus learned how to handle himself in a fight. Incredibly strong for his age, he quit school when he was fourteen and found a job on a labor gang in the shipyard. Demanding work, even for grown men, some of them resented the boy. One miserable bastard who'd been drinking at lunch hip-checked him off a catwalk, breaking the boy's arm above the wrist. Jimmy climbed back up ripping into the bully until the other men broke it up. He won broken arm and all. The grown man clearly got the worst of it; his nose flattened, and he was covered in his own blood.

Jimmy couldn't let his boss know he'd broken his arm. He taped it tightly, and went back to work and did everything asked of him. A job during the depression demanded a full day's work for a day's pay. The men knew the kid was hurt and afraid to show it. From then on, Johnny's dad was one of them. They honored him with the tag "Big Jim."

Every week he brought his pay envelope home and handed it to his mother, a widow raising two boys in difficult times. By 1941, when the war broke out, Big Jim had become the youngest foreman in the yard, in charge of thirty men. Married and the father of two little boys, he was kept out of the service with a legitimate military deferment for *work essential to the war effort*. Big Jim stayed home and built ships while others went to war. Haunted by missing out on something that defined his generation, Big Jim felt guilty that he stayed behind. He never got over it.

Almost every Friday night after the war, Johnny's uncles and some of Big Jim's old gang dropped by for poker and tossed down a few "cold ones." They called it an "all-night bull session." The men elbowed around the kitchen table, the top protected by a faded-yellow oilcloth pocked with cigarette burns. Wisps of smoke filled the air as the men drank home-made beer out of dark brown bottles. Johnny never forgot how those bottles felt when he dug them out of a galvanized wash tub and ran them in to the card players. Dripping wet, ice-water cold, the old glass surface covered with countless fine scratches as if it had been finely sandpapered. Running the beers in when his name was called, he'd slip back into the pantry hoping they'd forget he was there. Johnny loved their stories. These men, all good storytellers, laughed and drank, going on and on with tales that carried the night away. Some stories about ball games and crazy-ass things they'd done growing up made Johnny giggle.

But some stories took turns a six-year-old boy couldn't follow, things the men had seen and done in the war. He stood quietly, just out of sight, hungry for "grown up talk." His favorites were the wild, exotic stories of danger and adventure in faraway places with names he had never heard and couldn't remember. Big Jim's old gang lowered their voices when their talk turned to terrible, unimaginable things. Johnny felt his heart thump so hard he worried it would give him away. Sometimes the stories were funny, ending in fits of laughter, but often, the stories trailed into a hush, when the men could find no words to tell what they felt in their hearts.

As a small boy, Johnny came to understand that not being a part of what the others had seen and done cut through his father like a knife. Afraid the floor would creak, he waited hand over heart knowing what would come after one of these long silences.

Someone spoke. He wasn't sure who, but it was never Big Jim. It was the unquestioned mantra of toxic male folly, conflating good memories with bad and a sense that it all had something to do with becoming a man. The low, gravelly voice rumbled across the room confirming an almost universal male belief.

"God strike me dead; I wouldn't have missed it for the world."

Johnny vowed he would never be left behind. He would go to war. If his country needed him, he'd step forward. But a little boy is too young to grasp an unspoken truth. In card games and war stories, more often than not, a good bluff beats a better hand.

Tom Garvey

"I do not know how dreams arise but I know that if we meditate on a dream sufficiently long and thoroughly, if we take it about with us and turn it over and over, something almost always comes of it."

~ Carl Jung

A Mystical Burden

John McManus sold his candy apple red motorcycle to pay for his first year in college at an all-male military school near his home. Three years older than other freshman, he enrolled as a civilian day student. The only three women attending classes were two wives of professors and the head librarian's daughter. He fell in love with one of them. She was stunning, ten years older, and married to an English professor who was also his freshman guidance counselor. Unlike anyone he had ever known, it was as though her mind was like a castle with many doors and windows. One of the doors she opened for him was a curiosity about astrology. "You're a typical Gemini," she told him laughing. Though skeptical, John found everything she told him fascinating. Their love didn't work out. He should have seen it in the stars.

John walked out of an American History class one miserable, gray October morning after overhearing a kid who owned a new Corvette telling someone his father thought anyone with half a brain and money should never have to go to Vietnam. The entitled kid agreed with his father. The war was a good thing, for the economy and to stem Communism, but he shouldn't have to go. There were enough poor minority kids to fight this war. They had no future and, if idle, would only become a problem. The tipping point came when the kid said, "It would thin out the herd."

John thought of his father and how he missed out on his war. He thought of his own screwed up love life. He stood up and walked out of the room, leaving his coat and books on the desk. He walked away in a daze and wandered downtown in the rain, through the streets of Chester, to the Armed Forces Recruiting Office in the Post Office. He signed all the necessary papers, volunteering "Airborne, unassigned, Vietnam." When John came home that evening soaking wet, his Mother broke out laughing. "What in God's name happened to you? You look like something the cat dragged in." His Mother's legs buckled when he told her he joined the Army. Big Jim took it the hardest.

In the next few years, while training in North Carolina and Georgia, John stayed in touch with his former professor's wife. No longer lovers, they remained friends.

Home on leave, late January 1968, on one of his last days before leaving for Vietnam, he rode with her while she ran errands in a growing snowstorm. At a pharmacy, listlessly roaming the aisles while she waited to fill a prescription, he found himself in the magazine/book area. Hoping to find something to read on the twenty-hour flight only a few days away, he stared at magazine stories written for a world he was leaving.   Nothing interested him.

A paperback book caught his attention; *Gemini, 1968*, by Sydney Omarr, *A Day by Day Account of the Coming Year*. "Sweet suffering shit" escaped McManus so loudly heads turned his way. Self-conscious now, yet irresistibly drawn to a possible look into his future, he flipped to a random day in August, the 17th. Opening a book haphazardly in the middle was something a Gemini might do. None of what John read was good. The day called for *A mystical burden* of some sort. Reading more, *An unpremeditated act of courage,* and that he *would have to pass some cosmic test otherwise suffer some dire consequences.*

He jammed the book back in the rack upside down, then reached for it again, hand hovering in the air. The book reminded him that flying a flag upside down was a way to signal distress. He couldn't touch the book.   Muttering "It don't mean nothing" under his breath, John promised himself he'd never think about this again, nor ever mention the incident to anyone.

Days later, on a plane to California, the first leg of his journey to Vietnam, John McManus carried a concern he'd picked up in that bookstore he hadn't foreseen or wanted; a bad and recurring obsession with a far off day in August. He boarded the plane to war carrying something he never previously considered; a morbid premonition of some undefined consequence yet hanging in the stars.

Don't Mean Nothin'

In the first week of February 1968, John McManus waved goodbye to his family and buckled himself into his seat for the flight to San Francisco. It was strange being home this last time. "Goodbyes" carried a different weight. He wasn't the same person he'd been almost two and a half years ago when he'd gone into the Army. His family and friends felt the difference more than they understood the change. They wanted him to always be the John they loved and didn't comprehend that the boy they wanted to hold onto might not be able to survive what faced him. They didn't grasp he had already left them in ways they could never understand. He had become an "outsider" living in a far different world where their values could get him killed. It wasn't he didn't have the ability or desire to explain it to them. Their Johnny simply had no notion there was any reason to try.

They didn't understand who he had become and he didn't realize how much he'd changed. The seeds of post traumatic stress were sown before he ever left for Vietnam. If he returned, some part of him would certainly never come home. The young man waving goodbye could never come home. He might not die, but something in his soul would change. "Goodbye" meant something different for each of them.

Being home this last time hadn't been easy. He smiled, thinking that in the Army he was almost never referred to by his first name. Nobody bothered with it. He was simply "McManus," sometimes rank preceded his name, but often he was just some version of "that fucking McManus." Common use in the Army was just last names, the name on the name tag. He thought back to the training he'd had over the last few years and how lucky he was to have been so well-trained for whatever lay ahead. One of the first friends he'd made in the Army, Tony Garris from Baltimore, had been killed in Vietnam only a few months after Basic Training. The kid had almost no training at all. Tony was killed his first month in Vietnam. Thinking of Garris triggered guilty thoughts of all the training he'd had.

After Basic, McManus had applied for OCS, Infantry Officer's Candidate School, the first step in his plan to climb the totem pole. He needed to leapfrog past men like his sadistic platoon sergeant in Basic. The Army realized he was a "true believer" since he volunteered for everything possible. He had the good fortune to receive incredible training. He trained longer and harder than most guys going to Vietnam, well over two years. On days off he snuck onto the obstacle course and went on long runs deep into the pine barrens surrounding the military post.

McManus graduated from Infantry OCS as a 2nd Lieutenant and headed across Fort Benning to the airborne area. For the past six months, he'd watched men descend from the 250-foot jump

16

towers as he stood in the chow line outside the 92nd Company OCS mess hall. He hungered to be a paratrooper like one of his father's card-playing friends who'd parachuted into Normandy with the 101st Airborne. After Jump School, he headed up to Fort Bragg, North Carolina, assigned to the 6th Special Forces Group for further training. After reporting into C Company, 6th SF Group, he realized he'd hit the jackpot.

Assigned to a training detachment, his Team Sergeant was Master Sergeant Janus Rozanski who'd had his horse shot out from under him on September 1st, 1939, when his Polish Cavalry unit was ordered to charge German tanks crossing into his homeland on the first day of World War II. Horses against tanks didn't make much sense, but it was all they had. Seriously wounded, Rozanski crawled into the forest and became a legendary resistance leader in the Polish Home Army.

Rozanski came to America in 1948 seeking employment in the only line of work he knew. He joined the United States Army as a paratrooper. In the Korean War, Janus distinguished himself in an airborne unit. When Special Forces were founded by Aaron Bank and members of the OSS and CIA in the early 1950's, he was recruited into the small elite unit. Rozanski spent much of the next fifteen years in intensive training and helped write the book on unconventional warfare.

In his late forties when he met McManus in the spring of 1967, Janus Rozanski was considered an older man in the unit, but he could carry a heavy rucksack farther and faster than any of the men under his command. Janus sensed potential in his new team

saw someone he could work with in McManus.
e himself too seriously and understood he had
anski felt he could keep him from being clumsy
or rank and always aware of what hung in the
balance when he made decisions involving others' lives. He
instilled in his young Lieutenant a sense of always hungering to
learn *that one thing more* that might make the difference.

He had a raw hunger to learn all he could and Rozanski, the
master, trained his grateful student very well. McManus knew
he'd struck gold. He loved Janus. After five months of tutoring
by one of the most experienced and professional team sergeants
in Special Forces, he was assigned to the John F. Kennedy Center
for Special Warfare for the Qualification course, the "Q" Course.
Graduation after three months would qualify him as a Special
Forces Officer, the last step before going to Vietnam. Being
exposed to Rozanski's intense "on the job training" prior to
attending the "Q" course, gave McManus a "leg up" on many of
the courses, but he applied himself and visited Janus in their team
room at night to discuss deeper nuances of what he was learning.
They sat drinking coffee and sometimes Janus' "Polish martinis"
for hours. He graduated in early fall, 1967 and returned to
Rozanski and their team for three more months of even more
intensified training for he was now on orders for Vietnam.

During his time in North Carolina with Janus, almost all of his
parachute jumps occurred at night. McManus loved it all. Always
hungry for the respect of his team, a group of pretty bizarre men
even by Army standards, he always volunteered to jump with the
highly volatile blasting caps when they were required on field
training missions. Once when a "wind dummy" was needed

McManus stepped forward to be the first man out the door so the jumpmaster could calculate where to start the drop. He realized when he ended up on another drop zone miles from where he was supposed to be that the team had really pulled one on him. He took it in stride, never complaining. If anything, he was blasé.

Rozanski had molded his young lieutenant into a leader who understood his place on the team and would never ask anyone to do something he wouldn't do himself. Getting better and better at what he was doing, training in swamps in Florida and Georgia and the mountains of western North Carolina, stress, danger, hardship, and misery came to mean nothing. "Pas de quoi," *It is nothing,* he would say, quoting his master. He became comfortable in a world of hard men. He couldn't wait. He hungered for war. His war.

One thing that occurred in training bothered him. Old timers, who were seasoned veterans, occasionally told stories about guys with premonitions. Guys with things gnawing at them that too often came true. He realized it was always a worst case scenario for the poor son of a bitch holding the crystal ball. McManus told himself he wasn't going to play that game; he wouldn't be one of those guys fulfilling his own bleak prophecy. This premonition nonsense, a tango McManus refused to dance.

Reflecting on all he'd experienced in the Army, he flew west to California, quiet moments dragging him back to that incident in the drug store. He kept telling himself he wasn't the least concerned about August 17th and some clown named Sydney Omarr's crazy prediction. This denial collided point counterpoint with a growing awareness he refused to acknowledge or mention, an increasing obsession about the 17th. He reasoned if he didn't tell anybody, he wouldn't be like those other guys. If he kept this to himself, nothing would happen. Didn't much matter, asleep or awake, he became obsessed. The 17th crawled inside his head, made a nest, and fouled it.

McManus could still laugh at himself. He smiled remembering Walt Whitman, another Gemini, saying, "I contradict myself? Very well, I contradict myself. I am large, I contain multitudes." He dreamed of misty colors in wisps of angry air. Somehow a mix of colors worked its way into his visions of the 17th. He didn't know why or where this came from.

 He spent eleven hours in a hangar at Travis Air Force Base before transferring to a Military Charter for Vietnam everyone aboard in uniform, mostly Army. He sat next to a nervous kid, drafted into service. Praying aloud most of the way, the kid ordered milk every time the stewardess asked if he wanted anything. They had little to say to each other. McManus thought he was going to the greatest party ever, kind of a Mardi Gras in a free-fire zone where he could ply his military skills.

Some fool he trained with at Fort Bragg told him he was lucky to be going to Vietnam at the very end of January because of a big nationwide celebration called "Tet." The fool said it was like Mardi Gras but even better. Celebrated all over the country, Tet went on for a week. The war stopped while both sides danced, drank and partied. McManus, capable of being a fool in his own right, went along with this line of thinking. Caught up in a contagion of fools, he thought "Hell, Vietnam is going to be great!"

Both fools were right, but about the wrong thing. Tet turned out to be a great time for the enemy who launched the wildest balls-to-the-wall-all-out-surprise-attack of the war. Everybody in the country who hated the government, aged five to a hundred, rose up and went to work on a reception that flat-out ruined his Mardi Gras.

The plane landed so erratically it seemed to be crashing. Maybe the pilot overreacted, or maybe he was advised to land that way by the tower, but it was one highly dramatic entrance to war. The praying draftee threw up all over him as they landed hard, bouncing more than touching down, in a loud metal-wrenching lurch. McManus gagged on the smell of vomit-sour milk. The plane, braking radically, swerved, which prompted a loud outcry from everyone on board.

The pilot, panic in his voice, hollered over the intercom, "Stay calm, get off the plane. Run for it! Plane is a target! Run as far as you can." One stewardess stood behind the other crying. The stewardess closest to the door kept saying "I hate this fucking place, I hate this fucking place," instead of "Buh-bye." McManus passed her in a tangle of men fighting to get out the small door, more as if they'd crashed than landed. The crying stewardess offered, "Run!" as parting advice.

In the pushing and shoving, words like "Please step carefully," played on a now comic-tape in the background. A running panic started on the ramp. The milk-fed praying draftee fell forward, stepping on McManus' ankle. They all went down together, a parody of the Falling Domino Theory that brought them to Vietnam in the first place. He hit the ground, rolling over and over, in his vomit-soaked khakis. Rolling farther than necessary, to get away from the cursing rugby-like scrum of bodies at the bottom of the ramp, cinders and dirt clinging to his wet clothes. He felt like a secret recipe for a batter-dipped fool. Fires burned in the distance.

Taking off at a dead run toward a building 300 yards away, McManus looked over his shoulder at the plane. Braniff Airlines had painted a hip 1960's slogan in pastels that covered the entire side of their plane: *A different way to fly*. He ran into the shadows of the hangar under a giant "Welcome to Vietnam" sign, laughing as much in relief as ironic humor. He replayed an old newsreel image in his mind: Mac Arthur wading ashore in the Philippines, poised and starched, with an arrogant sense of self-importance. One minute in Vietnam taught him what anyone who has ever been to war knows: when it comes to actual combat, war becomes a crap shoot and all planning, training, or preparation "don't mean nothin'." Lieutenant John McManus slid down the wall beneath the welcome sign, thinking how the images of MacArthur and him, marching off to war, formed a paradoxically perfect double negative. That expression he'd ended up chanting in the drug store only last week summed it up, "Don't mean nothin'." Punctuated by far off explosions, McManus soothed himself with "Don't mean nothin', don't mean nothin'."

So John McManus didn't enter Vietnam confidently like a self-absorbed MacArthur. He arrived a rattled, panicked guy who woke up from childhood dreams of war in a vomit-soaked uniform to realize he was in over his head. After catching his breath, and limping gingerly from his fall from grace, he watched his plane taxi down the runway, trailed by an animated herd of men dragging duffle bags screaming fanatically to get aboard. Tet had erupted at the same time all over the country, but that was almost a week ago. He didn't know it that first night, but the explosions turned out to be mostly "friendly" outgoing artillery fire from a nearby firebase. Adrenalin wearing off, he felt exhausted as he crouched in a corner for protection. Falling asleep on the ground, appropriately curled in a fetal position, he closed his eyes, passing from one specific nightmare, his present life, to a hazy dream of an exact day in his future, August the17th. Sleeping without rest, he awoke without a clear image of where his dream might take him.

Juicy Fruit

About seven the next morning, no one seemed to be in charge of anything in the fenced off area of the airbase where they'd landed. Mass disorganization, no mess hall or place to eat, men milling around chain smoking and telling stories that made McManus wonder if they'd all come in on the same plane. It was "Rumor Central," and as time passed he heard tales grow so outrageous, he began to think some of these men hadn't spent the night on the same planet. He smiled as a bright blue Air Force Bus rolled up with two heavily armed Air Force Military Police riding escort. All the glass had been removed from the windows, replaced by heavy mesh screens covering the openings. One of the Military Policemen told them, "It's so the Viet Cong can't throw grenades into the bus." They were supposed to have met his flight last night, and though these MPs posed like a pair of John Waynes, they didn't have any idea what was going on or why the passengers had been left to fend for themselves overnight. Lieutenant McManus couldn't wait to get his hands on a loaded gun. These cocky rear-echelon MPs didn't inspire confidence.

The men ran like maniacs to the bus, pushing and shoving to get on. They filed onto the bus smelling like they'd spent the night in a dumpster behind a seafood restaurant. "Hurry up and wait," an old Army cliché, described their day perfectly. The sun rose, baking the bus. No air stirred. Not having any information, they waited, pissing and moaning, sharing rumors and stinking. Fear has an odor. Early afternoon they heard it was safe to go. Trip to be a *Milk Run*, safe to move, although the enemy had control of many major cities. Talk circulated about Viet Cong invading the American Embassy and raising their flag. Rumors circulated about rumors. The bus took them to the 90th Replacement Depot, the "Repo-Depo" for processing and assignment. The 90th turned out to be a tent city surrounding a core of temporary buildings in Ben Hoa near Ton Son Nhut airfield where they had landed. McManus heard that it normally would take a few days to go through the "Depo," but for them, it would take a week. Several nights running, firefights, real gun battles had taken place at the gate to the Replacement Depot. This had never happened before. Mortars and rockets had exploded all over the base, some near, some far, but nothing for the last two nights. The frantic men were told to relax, they were safe. Safe but unarmed. If the base were threatened, they'd be issued weapons. This is safe? No one believed it. For six long, cringing, unwashed, no-change-of-clothes days, he still hadn't gotten his hands on a weapon. Disheartening? Shit, piss, and corruption, this was the stuff of lawsuits. Under attack, at war, life threatened, barbarians at the gates, and the clowns who brought him here can't come up with a weapon. How screwed up can war get?

A story circulated about a kid on the bus that pulled out an hour after McManus'. The guy offered a stick of gum to one of his MP escorts when he got shot in the head. He was dead before the bus got him to a medic. His last words were "Juicy Fruit." The MP escort shot him. Leaning forward to take the offered gum, the Military Policeman's M-16 rifle went off. He shouldn't have had a round chambered with the safety off. It's all a fucking crap shoot! Take a seat, take a chance, and your immortal last words are "Juicy Fruit." The last things the hapless kid heard and saw as the gun exploded in his face, an MP smiling and reaching out saying "Thanks." The kid's mother, praying he'd come home as soon as possible, getting her wish, but not the way she wanted. Vietnam, a place where you couldn't tell real from rumor even if it occurred right before your eyes. He realized he'd stumbled off a plane into an unpredictably lethal *What the Fuck?* world. Alice's Wonderland, all logic and reality be damned. Down the rabbit hole we go.

Irony and the haphazard insanity of war tumbling around in his head, McManus caught himself smiling, thinking how war differed from the stories he'd heard as a kid. He thought of Kurt Vonnegut's young soldier in *Slaughterhouse Five*. What was his name? He tried to remember. It came to him in a flash: *Billy Pilgrim*! He mouthed Billy's words slowly "I realize that I am a very slow realizer." He thought that if his dreams about the 17th meant anything, he was somehow insured at least until mid-August. He had this strange feeling, comforted somehow by his premonitions, a weird insurance policy. He didn't want to know what the premiums cost.

War in Paradise

McManus was awake. He wasn't dreaming. It was a beautiful sunny day. Under a warm, soft blue sky he lugged a new duffle bag up the rear cargo ramp of a C-123, self-conscious that his much-too-green bag announced he's fresh meat. The plane, a fat body, twin-prop cargo plane, was like an old friend. He'd made countless night parachute jumps out of these babies over the past year. McManus settled into a mesh bench seat next to a man in faded jungle fatigues. The man nodded, muttering it would be a "Hop and drop." Not sure what the man said or meant, he nodded in return. They flew up the coast. Everybody a tourist, Instamatic cameras at the windows, white sandy beaches, waves along the shoreline. The old timer was right: up and down, fifteen minutes, plane descending. Cam Rahn Bay, world's largest natural harbor, a surfing paradise.

Loud hydraulic noises sounded as the ramp eased down onto the tarmac. An odor of oil, sweat, and coconut butter engulfed McManus as glaring sunlight flooded the plane. He squinted, everything blindingly bright. Like waking from a bad dream, war had gone away, replaced by guys working on their tans. Pressure off. Glistening bodies in cut-off shorts, sunglasses, baseball hats, Army and Air Force personnel intermixed, moving about, radio headphones and clipboards, shuttling fork lifts with cargo. Confident, calm, young men in charge, laughing, cutting up, and happily far from the jungle. Men shuffled onto the plane, dropping their gear, wiggling into a seat. Others drifted down the ramp into the sun, moving away. McManus squirmed in his seat, waiting. In twenty minutes, they taxied for takeoff to Nha Trang, their next stop. The man who spoke to him earlier, wearing the authority of faded fatigues, shouted, "Another hop and drop" over the roar of the unsound-proofed plane. McManus thought he'd said "Pop and drop" the first time. Man went on, "This time we cut out to sea, just around the mountains between Cam Rahn and Nha Trang, so we don't take fire. Might be twenty minutes at most." McManus only heard half of this, grinning stupidly, nodding like this was old news.

He'd get off at Nha Trang, Headquarters for the 5th Special Forces Group. They'd "in-process" him and send him inland, far into "Indian country." There'd been heavy fighting in Nha Trang all week. He would see war first hand. In Nha Trang there'd be action. McManus was excited. He still had no weapon, definitely a drawback, but he was jazzed. His time coming, feeling the beat, energized, alive. This would be it. This was what he'd volunteered for.

As the plane circled to land he pressed his face against a small window enjoying one of the world's most unforgettable sights, an old French colonial city beside the South China Sea. A tropical bay filled with lush little jungle mountain tops that rose to form small islands rising out of unimaginably blue water. White sand and palm trees lined the shore. On a steep hill overlooking the city sat a giant white Buddha looking philosophically down on a bougainvillea-colored war in paradise. Landing at a large air base they taxied to a cluster of older buildings from a time gone by. The engines feathered into silence. The ramp dropped. Loud noises, swirls of dust and pungent fruity odors, mingled with a hint of decay, flooding the plane. Life and death buzzed around like flies in strange, exotic air.

But still no war. McManus shouldered his bag, sauntering into blinding sunlight as casually as he could, walking onto a page torn from a Graham Greene novel, trying so hard to not be the new guy. He stared at a pattern of sporadic bullet holes. Some new, others very old, they pocked the faded red walls of the control tower and some weary hangars, a silent, though violent, story of then and now. In the shade of some dilapidated hangars, he observed a gumbo of mysterious characters, an odd mix of cultures wandering about, some furtive, others loud and cavalier, speaking staccato, sing-song Vietnamese or seductive French.

An ancient Vietnamese man, a bag of bones in tattered rags, knees and elbows akimbo, slumped against a wall in the hard-packed dirt. McManus keyed in on him, unable to look away. Everyone else ignored the man, moving around him as if he didn't exist.

The man held a string attached to the leg of a chicken. It hobbled on an injured leg, pecking the dirt, idling several feet away from the bony old man, moving to the end of its tether, the limit of its small world.

The man tugged the string. The chicken clucked chicken complaints, ambling gingerly back to its master. Tears ran down the old man's dusty face leaving a glistening trail, all life's hope beaten out of him.

McManus felt a word forming in his subconscious: *Pathos*. Comprehending its full emotional impact maybe for the first time in his life, feeling fully what he was seeing, somehow drawn into it. He wanted to approach the old man but couldn't. More than language separated him from this man's world.

Moving about, McManus saw Vietnamese everywhere. A strange mix of characters intermingled. Americans in civilian clothes, unaccountable, preoccupied as if starring in a movie of their lives. One man, all in black, absorbed by his reflection in a broken window, a legend in his own mind, so obviously loving what he saw, posing, drawing slowly and deliberately on a cigarette, "on camera." A squealing muddy pig ran loose through the scene chased by a giggling frenzy of children, a hysterical mother trailing.

McManus looked around, spotted two men in faded fatigues, green berets, no rank, insignias or name tags. He walked over to them and stood by their jeep parked near a gate. No one spoke, but one of the men nodded to him. He threw his bag in the back, climbed in after it. They took off on a bumpy, high-speed ride down side streets and through the rear gate of a large supply depot stacked two stories high with war material, a mountain of explosive grief for somebody. He held on as they skidded in a reckless blur out the back of the supply area and through another gate past swirls of rusting barbed wire. They slid to a stop in an area surrounded by Quonset huts and buildings ringed by sandbags, stacked chest high. Flags and banners hung limp, rippled by a heat mirage off the blacktop. A big sign announced "Headquarters 5th Special Forces Group, Vietnam." No secrets here, but not a soul in sight. He climbed out, dragging his duffle bag to the ground and thanked the men. The man in the passenger seat said, "Nobody's around, big cookout down on the beach." Driver added, "Welcome to come down after you sign in and stash your gear." While trying to thank them again, they drove off laughing at something they didn't share.

Drained of energy, soaking wet from the heat, he dragged his bag over to what had to be the main door. He stood in front of a plaque. Names of men killed. A long list, most recent deaths up until a few weeks ago, just before Tet. John McManus, recently promoted to 1st Lieutenant, shuddered imagining his name up there. The way things were going, he thought maybe it should just read "That fucking McManus - 8/17/1968."

"Don't do this to yourself," he thought, shaking his head. He went through the door. Inside, he reported to a duty clerk, feet up on a desk, who couldn't be bothered to look up from an old *Playboy*. McManus signed a roster book. Still not looking at him, the clerk mumbled, "Find an empty cot out back in the transient barracks, stash your stuff." He went out a rear door to another low building ringed by chest-high sandbags. He found a bed draped with mosquito netting, mattress, canvas mattress cover, but no pillow or sheets. Someone had slept in the bed with muddy boots. Under the bed, little tumbleweed balls of gray lint and one rumpled sock. He pushed his duffle bag underneath, swallowed a malaria pill dry, making a face. The pill bitter.

Going back to the front office, he asked the clerk where he could get a weapon. The *Playboy*-reading clerk seemed amused, looking at him for the first time. He spoke as if to a child, "You can't get a weapon. Armory's closed. Everybody's at the beach." McManus waited for more. This is war? The clerk went back to his magazine, spoke without looking up, "You can go to the beach if you want. Officers' club's open." He stared at McManus' Lieutenant's bars with contempt, "Somebody's probably there if you want a beer, something to eat. Massage parlor across the compound got closed down by the fucking Group Chaplain last week. If you want to get laid you have to go downtown." The clerk interrupted his reading long enough to tell how the Chaplain naively went for a massage and a woman asked him in pidgin English if he wanted "A good-happy-penis-wonder-joy." When he stammered, "No!" she asked if he'd rather have a boy. Chaplain went fucking nuts!

Prostitution fifty yards from the chapel, *What's war coming to?* McManus mused, as he wandered out into the compound. He didn't want sex or a cook out. He wanted a weapon and war. It crossed his mind something seemed fundamentally wrong with his values. He smiled. Standing in the middle of the big paved open square in front of the 5th Special Forces Group Headquarters, shit-eating grin on his face, John McManus took in the raw beauty surrounding Nha Trang like a little boy in a fantasy wonderland, the most beautiful place he'd ever seen. Long light green expanses of rice fields ran for over a mile before folding into foothills that blended into surrounding mountains hazed by soft blue mists of unpolluted sky. From the plane he'd seen an old French-style Indochinese city, white colonial buildings, bougainvillea and giant palm trees with lush dark green leaves everywhere, a busy harbor crowded with islands. They looked like mountain tops rising right out of the sea, too many to count, rising steeply, disappearing into the haze. Forbidding places ripe with lush tropical vegetation. This magnificent city of Nha Trang, ringed by all these exotic mysterious mountains. He'd never seen so many subtle shades of green. Mesmerized, he spoke softly to himself, "Not real war at all. It's a postcard."

He stood looking at the beautiful mountains, thinking somebody on the other side of all this, some enemy, who like him, may have just come here for the very first time, could probably be looking down on all this wonder. Someday life might bring them together, but not today. Not today. The war was on hold for some reason. McManus was tired. No, he was exhausted. Sleep at night hadn't meant rest. He felt his energy draining as he stood there. He needed rest. Maybe it was heat, maybe uncertainty. Without a weapon, he wasn't going anywhere. He went back to his cot, took off his boots, got under the netting and fell asleep still wearing one sock. Drifting off, he sensed he'd be lucky to defend himself from anything in this country, even the threat of being bored to death.

Confusion Now Hath Made Its Masterpiece

McManus slept fitfully, waking up in a cold sweat. He'd been dreaming about the 17th, and there'd been flashes of the plaque with the names of all those guys killed. What's this dream all about? What's gonna happen to me? What *might* happen he corrected himself, lacing up a jungle boot. His troubled dreams didn't leave clear images. From all the dreams, and there were many by this time, he obsessed on some connection to the biblical story of Joseph and his coat of many colors. Colors flooded his mind. Colors diffused, mixed, mingling together, colors dancing with each other, brilliant ribbons of color, a mesmerizing beauty. The dream had something to do with color, not a coat. What could color have to do with August 17th? "A magic coat," he thought, "I'm losing it, I'm in a war and can't even get a weapon!"

He sat on the edge of the cot, mosquito netting draped over his shoulders like a cape. In his dream, he sensed mist, maybe fog.

Never could identify the strange mix of colors. Always woke up the same way, chilled yet in a sweat, willing himself to not think about this floating, rolling panic of color and fear. One thing's certain; the dreams are clearly about the 17th. That astrology book triggered this! Beyond that and an obsession with mists of color, he had no idea what the dream meant.

Unsettled, he sat dwelling on a line from *Macbeth*. "Confusion now hath made its masterpiece." He thought "How wonderfully appropriate. How perfect the words." No matter how much he tried to keep it out of his mind, he found August 17th impossible to ignore. He'd carry it with him like a rifle, a hateful thing always at arm's reach, an obsessive dream more frightening than war. Preoccupation with death, a burden he didn't need to carry.

Lieutenant John McManus altered his fate while taking a piss. Waking from troubled sleep, tired and clammy, he went to a shed marked *Latrine* behind the barracks. Standing at a urinal that stank of sun-roasted urine, he met a man who changed his future. This guy, a lanky, raw-boned, Henry Fonda sort, stood at the urinal to his left, finishing up as McManus started to relieve himself. The stranger wore faded tiger-stripe fatigues, torn in places and covered with muddy clay and dried blood. His raggedy-ass jungle boots scratched and sun bleached almost white. He extended a hand to the man, "Name's John McManus. I got here three hours ago." Man looked at the extended hand, then at McManus' face, put a stick of gum in his mouth casually, nodded slow motion, studied him, said nothing. It could have been a scene from an old western. McManus went on. "Is that blood?" indicating the man's arm. Man looked at his sleeve as if noticing the blood for the first time. He shook McManus' extended hand with a look as though his thoughts were far away. When he spoke, he made a face as he realized he was somewhere he really didn't want to be. "The clerks and jerks runnin' this place see me looking like this, it's my ass." He went on, "These staff officers 'homesteading' desk jobs in Nha Trang hate field troops. I just missed catching a bird back to Pleiku. Now I'm stuck here till... maybe if I'm lucky, I hop a 'caribou' at dusk."

His name was Vernon K. Sutton. He was with the Pleiku Mike Force caring for some Montagnards wounded in a firefight on the border. "Montagnard" (the "g" is silent) was based on the French word for "mountaineer" and was the common term for the small, dark brown mountain people Special Forces hired as mercenaries and led on jungle operations up in the highlands. The nearest medical help available that Sutton trusted to care for his guy happened to be in Nha Trang. Sutton had been stranded in the headquarters area since early morning. He wanted out. McManus offered to buy him a beer. "Can I ask you some questions? Pick your brains?" Sutton looked around warily as if considering where he was, slowly nodding yes. "Nobody at the club, let's head over there. These starched assholes jump down your throat if they think you're from 'Indian country,' reminds them there's a war." He walked out of the latrine with Sutton. Away from the stench of the latrine, Sutton smelled ripe. Like war, not its rumor.

At the club, Sutton told McManus he'd come right from a hot spot out on the border aboard a Huey helicopter with a wounded Montagnard who'd taken a bullet for him. "My little guy saw the North Viet before I did, in a hole right in front of us, stepped right in front of me, took a bad one in the neck." Sutton stayed with him to make sure he wasn't sent to a Vietnamese hospital and ignored. He explained how the Vietnamese hate Montagnards and treat them like savages. He called them "Yards" and said though they were indigenous to Vietnam they were not Vietnamese at all but from a completely different ethnic stock, about the same size as Vietnamese but darker and more muscular. Sutton much-preferred Yards to Vietnamese he neither trusted nor respected. When the American hospital in Pleiku couldn't take his Yard, he cajoled the flight crew into a night in Nha Trang, which they didn't mind at all. Sutton got his Yard into the American-run hospital and stayed with him till he knew he'd be taken care of, well taken care of. "Little fucker's gonna make it," he said, raising his beer can in salute. "If I'd sent him off on his own he'd be lying on the floor of some Vietnamese hospital in Pleiku until he bled out. They'd toss him on a pile, leave him to be burned. Vietnamese don't even touch Montagnards." He got a faraway look, "Me, I love the little fucks."

They drank all afternoon. McManus was a sponge for Sutton's ocean of tactics and stories. He respected McManus for wanting to get out into the field and his willingness to learn anything he could. He'd fallen into calling McManus "Macca" after the second or third beer. Sutton had some "Aussies" on his team, and they called anybody with the a name that began with a Mc or Mac: *Macca.* McManus loved it. He felt so *not the new guy* hanging out with grungy Sutton and being called Macca in the Officer's Club in Nha Trang.

Sutton's voice was strained. He hadn't gotten much rest. The firefight in which the Yard had taken a round for Sutton had gone down on the Cambodian border not far from a new A-Camp, Ben Het, northwest of Kontum. Sutton assured McManus the camp's not long for this world if "Charlie" has anything to say about it. "Victor" and "Charlie" were the phonetic letters to spell "VC," short for Viet Cong. The common name for the enemy simply shortened to "Charlie." Ben Het had been mortared every night, and they got into firefights every time anyone ventured outside the wire. Enemy units were massing in the area. "Camp isn't nearly finished. Anybody tells you Ben Het has any chance, they're bullshitting you, don't believe them, Macca, don't trust them." Sutton told him the camp was under the operational command of B-24 in Kontum, northwest of Pleiku. "They're plugging holes in the team now, replacing at least three men, one got killed, one badly shot up, and one lucky bastard is going home intact. Don't go there!"

He looked at McManus and frowned. Sutton intuitively could see an innocent hunger, another new guy out to earn his spurs. The anger in his voice shook McManus by surprise. "Listen to me! Macca, you think you know what you're doing, you've trained long and hard. Macca, you really don't know shit!" He looked at McManus, exasperation in his raspy voice, "Listen to me! Hear what I'm telling you! John Wayne is total bullshit! Nothing but bullshit! Never wore a uniform that didn't come from the wardrobe department. All of us grew up on his crap. That's all it is! Listen to me. It's ingrained in us. Stop kidding yourself. Most of us got sucked into this for the adventure and maybe to see how we measure up. Every one of us thinks nothing bad will ever happen to them. That gets you started into the nightmare but eventually you end up battling like hell for your buddies. You end up fighting for them."

McManus stared at him. He hadn't seen this coming. Sutton's frustration came out like a teacher telling a not-too-bright-student what's going to be on an upcoming test, knowing that even with the answers, the student might fail.

Sutton plowed on. "First you think something bad can't happen to you. Then you realize it could. And then, if you are really astute, if you have your head out of your ass and have somehow survived, you realize, if you keep running border ops, it not only *can,* but *will* happen to you!" He looked at McManus who didn't move, a deer in the headlights. Sutton's voice softened, "It's okay to be scared. It's normal; it's human. Watch out for the guys who aren't scared. They don't get it." McManus could feel his heart beating. "You are going to meet some of the best people you will ever have the good fortune of knowing but you will also meet some of the worst. Don't judge guys by what they tell you they *think* they are doing. Watch them carefully. You'll *see* what they're really all about. Unfortunately, you never know the full truth utill your coals are in the fire. A lot of the best guys you'll ever meet aren't gonna make it out alive. Keep your eyes on the ball."

In a low voice, Sutton spoke. "Three things will keep you alive. Know where you are.

Know who you're with."

He lowered his eyes to the bar.

He spoke slowly, voice almost a whisper. McManus leaned in to hear. "And no matter what, Macca, and I don't know why I have such a strong sense this somehow applies to you, but I do.

Stay the fuck away from Ben Het."

Sutton's late evening flight didn't come off. He turned in early. When McManus looked for him in the morning, he found an empty space where Sutton's rucksack and rifle had been. McManus realized he had no idea what Sutton's rank was. He could have been a captain or a buck sergeant. No one in Special Forces wore any kind of insignia on their tiger fatigues, and the topic had never come up. Fresh mud from Ben Het on the mattress cover, Sutton slept with his boots on. Months later he heard Sutton lost a leg on a hot landing zone, couldn't confirm it, never knew if it was true.

Heaven Knows What

Assigned to Company B, 5th Special Forces, McManus caught a ride on a C-123 heading to Pleiku for further assignment. An afternoon flight, always the worst because the heat-thinned air made for a bumpy ride. The plane carried lumber, rice, and crates of nervous chickens who'd never flown before. Chicken shit, feathers, and a general stench filled the air. Trying to act savvy, McManus didn't pull it off. He threw up twice.

Pleiku, a hundred and forty-some miles northwest of Nha Trang, was a major helicopter base just over forty miles from the Cambodian border. God forsaken, Pleiku had swollen to five times its size of only a few years ago, ringed with cardboard and tin refugee shacks like a house of cards. Most trees were gone. There was little or no grass, leaving sun-scorched dust from the dry red clay, lying like thick silt everywhere. Hovering helicopters created nightmarish red clouds that drifted up into the sky creating a pink mist. Pleiku marked an ancient crossroads of silk, salt, and opium trade routes that ran from the South China

Sea to Cambodia, and from the Delta, north through the Central Highlands all the way to the Great Wall of China. In this red bowl of dust sat the headquarters of Company B, 5th Special Forces Group. Pleiku also housed one of the largest, angriest nests of war helicopters in the world.

McManus "in processed" again, for the third time now, and another studiously indifferent clerk told him to find a bunk, stash his gear and wait. In a few days someone would make a decision and pass him down the food chain for further assignment at some generic hell hole, to be named later, that would one day make him look back and long for the safety of Pleiku. Each step took him farther into "Indian country," where some legendary battles had taken place farther from civilization than he'd ever imagined. Pleiku sat less than forty miles from the site of the most disastrous battle of the war. It occurred a little over two years earlier in the Ia Drang Valley and would remain the greatest loss of American life in a 72-hour period in one location for the entire war. No other battle came close. The Army still hadn't issued him a weapon. Sweet suffering shit!

McManus stashed his bags on another dirty bunk and then wandered out into the center of the small cluster of buildings. Company B had a large inner courtyard with something he never expected. McManus stared in amazement at the reflection of pink clouds in the red dust colored water. They had a god damned swimming pool!

There was no one anywhere in sight. There was no life guard, only a lopsided sign cautioning: "Swim at your own risk." He shook his head, why not go for a swim? No rifle, no war.

Smiling, he put on shorts, grabbed a green towel and dove through a layer of red silt. Like everything America tried in Vietnam, the end result corkscrewed into something unforeseen. He climbed out of the pool, his body coated with thick, wet, red paste. Like oil-based paint, it didn't come off. McManus looked like a blue-eyed American Indian. When he went for a beer, the man behind the bar, clearly enjoying himself, said, "I see you've been in the pool." Coated red, McManus felt green.

Pleiku had milk, all the milk you could drink. He remembered the kid who sat next to him on the flight from California always asking for milk.

McManus could get fresh milk. He still couldn't get a weapon. He spent three days in Pleiku, drinking milk, swimming, learning to push the red silt away. At night, he listened to war stories at the bar and watched movies. On the third day, summoned to an assignment interview with the colonel who commanded Company B, McManus wandered over to his office after a greasy lunch to find out where his next assignment in II Corps would take him.

Seven young lieutenants sat around the Orderly Room waiting. McManus was the sixth man to have his name called to see the Commanding Officer. The orderly typing at the desk stopped and whispered behind his hand to McManus as he had done with every man who had gone before. The clerk's face strangely serious, considering his message: "Whatever you do in there, don't click your ball point pen if you have a retractable one." McManus must have given him an "Are you kidding me?" look. The typist added knowingly, "It drives Colonel Hobson mad," explaining, he'd thrown a stapler at a lieutenant who did it the other day. "Hates lieutenants," he said turning back to his hunt-and-peck typing. McManus kept his pen in his pocket. Thought to himself, driving this colonel mad would be a short commute. Taking a deep breath, he knocked on fate's door.

The interview was brief, six or seven minutes at most. McManus sat in front of the colonel, who continually clicked his ball point pen absent-mindedly. McManus reasoned he wouldn't have considered anything as unusual had the scene not been set up by the typist the way it had. He found himself enjoying the incongruous madness of his war. The *All the milk you can drink but no guns today, pen clicking, Catch 22, Magical Fucking Mystery Tour of Vietnam*. Who could have ever dreamed up such happy horseshit floated across his mind as he found himself hearing each of the colonel's clicks echoing like a thunderclap.

Struggling not to let his face give him away, like not laughing inappropriately at a funeral when something strikes you funny, he found himself fascinated by this colonel. A ferret-faced man with pocked skin, the colonel had large nostrils on a beak of a nose that looked like a can opener. The hair in his nose looked like cotton. How could he breathe?

McManus wasn't listening to a thing the rambling, whacked-out, pen-clicking colonel said. Trying not to laugh in his face, he kept a running tally of clicks: thirty-seven, thirty-eight... on and on. Vietnam, madness and the totally unexpected, the clicking colonel apparently par for the course. McManus, loving it, sat up when he heard the words "Bet Het" floating in a haze of clicks. "That's the new A-team out of Kontum, or you could go down to Ban Me Thuot for heaven knows what."

McManus knew from nights at the bar; that Ban Me Thuot, pronounced "Bammy-two-it," had been overrun and occupied for a week during Tet. The NVA, the North Vietnamese Army, had captured South Vietnamese Army tanks and used them to occupy downtown for more than five days. McManus had completely lost count of the number of pen clicks. He thought of Sutton, then Ben Het, cleared his throat, and said, "Give me 'heaven knows what,' Sir." The colonel clicked his pen again, wondering what McManus meant, staring distractedly across the desk. Blinking as if pulled back into the present, he said, "Okay, you're off to Ban Me Thuot." McManus stood, saluted, and bolted out the door, passing the last lieutenant in the waiting room being given his "Don't click your pen" briefing. He later learned Colonel Hobson sent the poor bastard to Ben Het, the only horse left in his stable.

John McManus stood on a helipad at first light looking to hitch a ride with anything flying south to Ban Me Thuot, some ninety miles to the southwest of Pleiku. Teddy Roosevelt was said to have stayed in the Emperor's hunting lodge in Ban Me Thuot back in 1909, hunting big game. The mountain jungles were still full of tigers as McManus flew over them. Ban Me Thuot, a quaint

French city, on the border in every sense of the word, was much closer to Cambodia than Pleiku and as near to the edge as you could get without being on an A-team. B-23 was the administrative and supply team in charge of the nine A-team outposts in lower II Corps, four right on the border, the others inland. The B-23 compound was headquartered in Ban Me Thuot in the actual shadow of the Emperor's obscenely large hunting lodge where Roosevelt stayed. The lodge, though rustic in some ways, was incredibly plush, built on the backs of laborers over sixty years ago. If they were paid anything at all, they would have been lucky. Even in 1968, the locals lived on family incomes equivalent to less than $50 in US currency per year.

It took McManus another week to in-process at B-23 because so many key staff officers who should have been there were away. Everybody seemed to be out of town. How do you pull that off, he wondered. He never figured out the *how* but he came to understand the *why*. Ban Me Thuot was probed by the enemy and mortared every night.

He also realized quickly that being stationed in Ban Me Thuot would be a kiss compared to the next rung down the ladder of the food chain where he'd soon be heading.

Assigned to an A team, Operational Detachment A-231, known as Tieu Atar, *Johnny got his gun.* B-23 finally issued him a rifle, an old WW II carbine, a puny little thing. The armorer told McManus he'd be issued an M-16 when he reached his team. He'd be heading north again, a little more than half way back towards Pleiku but farther west, much closer to the Cambodian border.

Tieu Atar, about forty-five miles west-northwest of Ban Me Thuot, sat just below the Chu Pong Massif, a cluster of granite mountains honeycombed with enemy caves straddling the Vietnam-Cambodian Border. This enemy sanctuary, close to the Ho Chi Minh trail formed the southern side of the Ia Drang Valley. Looking at the exact location on a large topographical map, he silently mouthed the words, "Holy shit!"

McManus heard some horrific stories about the Ia Drang Valley when he was up in Pleiku. He thought he had been moving away from the horrors of that area when he traveled south to Ban Me Thuot. Now, assigned to the northernmost camp supported and supplied by B-23 he'd be much closer to the Ia Drang Valley than when he'd been farther north in Pleiku.

He was heading into this area in the spring of 1968. It certainly had a violent history. In mid-November 1965, the First Air Cavalry darkened the sky with helicopters in the first major combat helicopter assault of the war. The Cav was out to test the tactics they had developed for this new kind of helicopter war. In multi-battalion strength augmented with several artillery fire bases air lifted in for support, The Cav began a three-day battle at the now infamous Landing Zone X-ray on the north side of the Chu Pong Massif. What they didn't realize when men from the first choppers ran into the razor-sharp elephant grass was that three regiments of North Vietnamese regulars were also eager to test their tactics against this new kind of air assault. No combat operations had ever gone this close to the border before 1965 and when they did it was a disaster. The battle was catastrophic, and literally, thousands of Mothers on both sides paid the ultimate price: their children would never come home alive. No operations of any significance would ever go back into the Ia Drang Valley other than recon missions by small Special Operations teams.

On the south side of Chu Pong Mountain was the northern edge of A-231's "AO," or Area of Operations. The Vietnamese called the Ia Drang area: "The Valley of a Thousand Ghosts."
When it came to estimating the head count of a crowd of ghosts McManus thought they weren't very good. The actual number must have been higher given the combat there. The 1st Air Cavalry suffered over three hundred soldiers killed in action in only seventy-two hours. The North Vietnamese easily lost ten times that many. Boys who had grown up all over America and parts of Northern Vietnam were gone to dust. The numbing pain their Mothers felt would live with them down all their days.

Recent aerial reconnaissance and electronic surveillance devices planted by a long range patrol from Special Operations showed a great increase in large enemy units infiltrating into Vietnam on the southern side of the mountain in early 1967. A-231's camp had been placed on the south side of the Chu Pong in the middle of this area of increased enemy activity. It was the closest camp south of the Ia Drang. Due east of Tieu Atar, almost the same distance from A-231 to landing zone X-ray, was the site of the last major battle of the French Indochina war fought in July of 1954 *after* the French defeat at Dien Bien Phu. The Chu Dreh Pass ambush was the site of the slaughter and complete destruction of an entire elite French unit, designated Mobile Group One Hundred. McManus realized he was moving into a historically bad neighborhood, extremely "dangerous ground."

Of the nine A-sites supplied and supported by B-23, Operational Detachment A-231 seemed to have the darkest future. Combat engineers had abandoned the camp before finishing their work. One of them left so quickly he forgot to take his M-16. Odds at the "Moose's Lounge," the bar in B-23's compound in Ban Me Thuot, were five to one A-231 wouldn't last through its first monsoon season. McManus wondered how B-team barflies could possibly know or not know what was really going to happen out on the border. Didn't really matter, Tieu Atar was no better than Ben Het. McManus realized Colonel Hobson had actually given him no choice at all.

He caught a ride on an Air America C-47, the old reliable "gooney bird," the same type of plane that dropped paratroopers in Normandy on D-Day. He'd hooked up with the crew at the Moose's Lounge in Ban Me Thuot the night before. "Air America" was the secret-not-so-secret CIA-run airline everybody seemed to know about. The pilot offered McManus a ride as a favor. Said he was "Sort of going that way" and they'd list him on the manifest as 70 kilos of rice, not as a passenger which for whatever reason wasn't authorized. McManus thanked them, shrugged, and threw his bags on board, muttering "Don't mean nothin'." They were just jerkin' him around. He didn't care. A ride was a ride. As the unmarked old bird labored down the runway, groaning into the sky, the sun came up. Heading farther into the mountains, moving northwest towards the Cambodian Border, McManus looked down on the mystical Highlands still wrapped in an eerie fog. The tops of dark green mountains reached up to him through the mist. The dense jungle in the valleys hidden and forbidding. He sensed these mountains held the secret of his dream.

Death Row

In less than a half an hour, the C-47 dropped dramatically into the low-hanging clouds. The airstrip was so short and cratered McManus thought they might crash into the jungle. The crew chief found his discomfort amusing as he threw his bags out the door and hollered "Jump!" McManus hesitated. The crew chief screamed "Now!" He dove out the door. Within thirty seconds, the plane turned, taxied, and took off, disappearing into the clouds, heading west to enter Cambodian airspace illegally. Brushing himself off, wondering what the hell happened, he stood next to his small bags in the brush where runway gave way to jungle. A bare-chested sergeant with the stub of an unlit cigar clenched in his teeth came roaring out of the jungle in a jeep. The jeep skidded to a stop, almost hitting him. He jumped in. The sergeant looked at his little carbine with contempt. First words of welcome: "Put the safety on, clear the round from the chamber." In a lurch, they took off bumping down a washboard road to camp.

McManus' new team, Operational Detachment A-231, was commonly referred to as *Tieu Atar* after the nearest most prominent terrain feature, a mountain just twelve klicks north in the foothills of the Chu Pong Massif. The area of operations this team was responsible for was almost square covering forty kilometers, generally north-south along the Cambodian border and from the border inland east a little over forty-two kilometers. A kilometer, colloquially known as a "klick" was six-tenths of a mile, so the team's area of responsibility was roughly twenty-four miles by twenty-four miles square. The camp sat in a fork in the Ya Hleo River flowing east from Cambodia into Vietnam. The fork in the river was formed where the larger Ya Hleo flowed north of the camp, and the smaller Ya Soup branched off flowing south of the camp. The "Y" fork the rivers formed sat almost dead center in A-231's area of operations and less than twenty "klicks," about twelve miles, from the Cambodian Border, commonly called the "red line" from its marking on the map. It was a "red line" in more ways than one.

The A-team's basic mission was border interdiction. Go out on small operations and make contact with any North Vietnamese units coming into Vietnam from the Ho Chi Minh trail just across the border. Stir something up, hopefully with a surprise ambush, then pray for air support. Run like hell through the jungle when there's no help coming. If an operation was being chased by a superior force, booby traps and stay behind ambushes could slow them down.

A-team operations were too large to hide and too small to go toe-to-toe against large NVA units rolling in from Cambodia. The Montagnards had little training and were severely under-armed with puny carbines. Only the two American Special Forces advisers leading these operations carried M-16s. This often proved a disadvantage in a firefight as the M-16s distinct sound gave away their location during a battle. The focus of attack always shifted onto the Americans because they had the radio. Take out radio contact, and you take out helicopter gunships and the only edge these small units could hope for. In almost all ways it was insane. Just a bunch of crazy Americans rolling the dice. Special Forces men kept taking these risks because most of them thrived on living on the very edge. They didn't have to be out there. Every last one of them had volunteered for this life.

The jeep driver's name was Wiley. He was the team's only radioman. The team should have had two but was short a medic also. Only Duc Lap, Buon Bleck and maybe one or two other camps operating under B-23 were fortunate enough to have two medics at that time, and at least one of them had a medic due to rotate home soon. Tieu Atar had opened just before last Christmas, in December 1967. Enemy contact was so intense, the engineers building the camp happily left during Tet, not having to come back. Official reports said the camp had been finished in record time, two months early, neglecting to mention that the engineers had been pulled out before the job was done. Damage during Tet to major bases and cities inland gave engineers an excuse to pick their assignments. Defenses at the camp seriously incomplete, Tieu Atar wasn't prepared to survive a prolonged attack.

Wiley's strange taste for gallows humor summed it up simply, "We're bait on the hook." He laughed. "I call the border camps 'Death row'." He saw the border camps as early warning devices, like smoke detectors for the flames of madness consuming Vietnam. McManus had come to the end of the line, bringing his obsession with August 17th with him.

A full Special Forces A-Team called for 12 men: two officers, and ten enlisted men. By the summer of '68, many teams were seriously under strength. Tieu Atar had only eight team members including McManus, their new, untested Commanding Officer. They were short a team sergeant, medic, communications-radio man, and a light weapons man. Hank, the intelligence sergeant, was acting team sergeant till Courtenay, the actual team sergeant, got back from emergency leave in the states.

The rank structure was unlike anything in any other unit in any army. Officers might write a report, plan an operation, run a border operation, cook lunch or dig a ditch. Everyone pitched in, no one wore regulation uniforms, and only shaved if an incoming plane or helicopter might have some pain-in-the-ass VIP on board. Most of the men lived in or near the team house, a small building, its walls burrowed into the earth with only the peaked tin roof showing, the lower edges of the roof almost sitting on the ground, with no more than 18 inches of screen for ventilation between the roof and ground.

The Inner compound also had an underground ammo bunker nearby, but deliberately not too close to the commo shack, a radio room with two often cantankerous 10-kilowatt diesel generators for power and the radio lifeline to Ban Me Thuot and the outside world. The inner perimeter also had an outhouse and a 4.2-inch mortar that could throw a big round about 6500 yards into the jungle. A four-foot-high fighting berm surrounded the inner perimeter so the team could hold out like the Alamo should the camp be overrun. Inside the outer perimeter, there were eight, much larger versions of the team house for the Montagnard "strike force" in four pairs of buildings, each pair coming together at a 45-degree angle to each other forming a point.

Overall the camp wasn't as large as a football field, and from the air, it looked like a large star with four points, a copy of the old Foreign Legionnaire's star-shaped camp. The Camp was home to a "Strike Force" of four hundred something Montagnards, and a twelve man Vietnamese Special Forces A-team who didn't seem to want to do anything but stay in camp and drink. In their defense, they were in this war for as long as it lasted and unlike the Americans couldn't go home after a one year tour. Three of the older men on the Vietnamese team had been fighting for the French against the Viet Minh in the early 1950's when McManus was in Cub Scouts.

Rounding out the camp were five interpreters. One spoke good English, two spoke confusing and poor English, the fourth spoke dangerously confusing English, and the last spoke almost no English at all, but he could cook like a demon, and that was the only reason he was on the payroll. All in all, never more than four hundred and fifty men lived inside the little star made out of rusting barbed wire.

The American public never had a clear grasp of what the camps were all about. The four hundred-some soldiers in the camp, with the exception of the small band of Special Forces volunteers and their Vietnamese Special Forces counterparts, were all mercenaries. They were not in the Army of South Vietnam nor, in almost all cases, were they even Vietnamese. Tieu Atar was fortunate their "strike force" was 100% Montagnard, mostly, but not all, from the Rhade (Rah-Day) tribe. American Special Forces universally preferred all-Montagnard camps to mixed camps with some Vietnamese.

Montagnard was a French term loosely translated "Mountain Man." These Highland natives had almost always lived in or close to the jungle. Prior to the French, they had avoided interaction with the Vietnamese and also had little or no contact with Western civilization. If asked who they were, the "Yards" as they were commonly called by Americans, after they got past total confusion as to why anyone would ask such a question, would simply explain "They were *the people*."

They weren't the rivers or sky or animals, they were the people. Wasn't it obvious? What a silly question! Anthropologists or academics might argue over labels, but it wasn't anything to which the people living in the Central Highlands gave much thought. If anything divided them into tribes, it was their different languages.

Vietnamese considered them less than human and would demean them as *Moi*, a derogative term translated as *wild men* or *savages*. Special Forces Intelligence sources estimated at least 3 to 5% of any "strike force" should be considered possible VC sympathizers but in an all-Montagnard camp, the number could be much lower or almost non-existent. The Yards loved the wild, outrageous characters drawn into Special Forces. This love flowed both ways. Most men in Special Forces loved the Yards implicitly, while for equally sound reasons, disliking and distrusting Vietnamese.

The money paid to the Montagnards wasn't much in American currency, much less than what a paperboy back in the states might make, maybe the equivalent of fifteen United States dollars a month, plus food, clothing, and a place to sleep in a camp the North Vietnamese were trying to obliterate. As Special Forces legend Jerry "Mad Dog" Shriver once said, "Just one good deal after another." Funds for these CIDG (Civilian Irregular Defense Group) operations came from an unaccountable part of the CIA budget and did not show up as part of the cost of the war. Speculation based on unfounded rumors favored an idea the money was cleverly laundered, somehow disappearing from cooked books in a CIA run computer, rumored to be on the third floor of an innocuous office somewhere in Oakland, California.

The Montagnards were simply good people who had lived in the Highlands for as long as they could remember and who merely wanted to raise their children, hunt, farm their fields, and revere their ancestors. They tried to mind their own business, but the war came and found them. They became cheap war labor for everybody who came into their mountains no matter how good anyone's intentions. The French came back into the Highlands after World War II, rebuilt their rubber, coffee and tobacco plantations, and fought the Viet Minh who didn't believe the French were entitled to the land. The Viet Minh were nationalists as well as communists. The French were Imperialists.

Missionaries arrived with the French and were essentially on their side.

Two weeks after arriving at Tieu Atar, McManus heard the situation explained honestly and succinctly when he passed through the only Montagnard village anywhere in his Area of Operations. McManus was on his first operation, and the village of Buon Ya Soup was about sixteen klicks south-east of Tieu Atar on the banks of the Ya Soup.

As he sat rubbing blistered feet and picking off leeches, plump with his blood, he listened as a Montagnard chieftain told him as they shared an extremely precious beer the old man had dug up from a hiding place in the clay floor under his jungle hut, "When men who look like you came they brought great death. We trusted them. They knew things we did not." McManus watched the chief search for words to explain his unabashed awe for the first white-faced men to arrive in the highlands. The chief smiled as he summed it up, "They came from the sky. Like great birds, they could fly."

He said this in a mixture of crude French and his own Montagnard language, a small piece of red clay from the beer bottle hanging from the edge of his lip. The chief had saved this beer for a special occasion. It was a generous offering. McManus was highly aware of its value. This beer had come to this moment having been carried overland through the jungle on the back of an elephant all the way from Ban Me Thuot, a hell of a rough trek, easily 70 kilometers. He had dug it from its hiding place and offered the first drink to McManus as though he were a visiting dignitary.

The import of this gesture settled on McManus as words, understanding, and the bottle passed back and forth between the young American and the village leader until the old man felt McManus comprehended what he meant. The Chief was sorry men who looked like McManus had ever come to his mountains. To McManus, this was a profoundly sobering insight. Direct communication distilled to one harsh message: The chief respected McManus but wished they had never met.

McManus soon crossed the line. Living with the Montagnards, running seat-of-the-pants operations on the highland trails with them, a man either got the hell out or became one with their spirit. The Yards would say, "I love you too much," using the word "too" when they meant "very." The literal translation was unintentionally extremely accurate. They did love the Americans "too" much. As crazy and wild as men drawn into Special Forces could be, most returned this love. The Montagnards were the most beautifully pure human beings McManus had ever known. They were sweet innocent children caught up in a sour, cynical war.

What McManus had to learn, what he really had come into the South Central Highlands to experience and still didn't understand, was a lesson only Montagnards could teach him, if only he could open himself to what they offered. A school bell was ringing for McManus, still too blocked to hear the knell of parting opportunity.

The young soldier's growth as a human being would begin when he finally grasped the Montagnard's belief in the power of dreams. Because of his fears surrounding August 17th, McManus held firmly to a vested interest in fighting this belief. But every morning the Montagnards gathered around a fire as a family to share stories about visions that visited them in the night.

Squatting in a circle, these people with no sense of an alphabet or written history would vividly describe their dreams and plan their day accordingly. Besieged by thoughts of August 17th, McManus didn't need this. He loved the Yards. They were opening his heart and mind even in war but this "dream thing" created a tug of war between his soul and sanity. McManus came to understand, if he really did have a date with his shadow on the 17th, he had to come to grips with his obligation to others who might get sucked into it. A line from Yeats' tortured him: "In dreams begins responsibility."

McManus' philosophy of life came from a deep love of literature and a stubborn Irish streak that a man could deal with a problem by not dealing with it. Ignore it, and it will go away. It had always been the only way he knew. "It's all in your mind" he kept telling himself. Sleep with the lights on. Pretend nothing is hiding under the bed. But on a deeper level, he sensed something out there.

He shook his head, thinking of Sidney Omar's prediction for the 17th, *"Mystical burden my red Irish ass!"*

Everything They Had

From that snowy day in the bookstore back home last January when McManus opened the book of astrological predictions, continuing all through the monsoon rains and heat of late July, he had been cursed with dreams about August 17th. He clearly wasn't winning this one. There had already been two dramatically disturbing occasions when Montagnards came to him with frightening dreams that later came true. His own dream simply wasn't going away. August 17th was getting closer. Like the Montagnards, he began to plan his future based on a dream.

He couldn't get away on R & R or down to Nha Trang in mid-August because the team was still too short of men. They had gained a light weapons man, Sergeant First Class Diggs who seemed to be fitting in well but medics and commo men were at a premium because their training back in the states took so long. Only a few teams McManus knew of had the luxury of two medics.

Because there was still only one commo man and one medic at Tieu Atar, neither was allowed to leave camp. Both Wiley and Tyre, the medic, wanted to go out on operations like everyone else and earn their spurs. But this rule from Nha Trang was non-negotiable. They could not leave the site under any circumstances unless they found a qualified medic or commo man to baby sit their camp while they were out in the jungle.

McManus, as team leader, stayed up most of one-night planning operations for August. He decided it would be better for the greatest number of others if he went out on an operation instead of remaining in camp. If something bad did happen on the 17th, at least the Montagnards' families living near the camp wouldn't get caught in the crossfire. Had he been certain something would actually happen that day, he would have felt obligated to slip through the wire and disappear into the jungle alone, dragging his fate with him.

McManus held firmly to the hope that his secret obsession was something he could alter if only he could come to grips with whatever his mystical burden was. He kept feeling he had been forewarned for a reason. He also felt the answer was right in front of him, but he couldn't see what it was. He was correct on both counts.

Word had come down through situation reports that an observation post less than a kilometer outside the wire at Ben Het had been hit hard. Two American Special Forces soldiers had either been killed or captured. Details were sketchy, but one of the soldiers was a sergeant first class, the other might be a lieutenant. It gave him an uncomfortable, bittersweet feeling. Relieved he'd met Vern Sutton and been warned to avoid Ben Het, he felt bad for this lieutenant. He felt like he had cheated on a test. McManus remembered the man's name, that last man to go see the colonel in Pleiku. He was pretty certain the guy's last name was Leonard. McManus felt sick. He hoped it wasn't Leonard.

Other pressures were building. Reliable intelligence sources revealed the high probability of a major North Vietnamese offensive late in the summer as the Presidential elections gained momentum. It was to be an all-out suicidal attack against a Special Forces border camp, overwhelming and holding the camp for several days to traumatize American voters into voting for peace. Normally the enemy would avoid attacking and holding terrain because of the enormous casualties. This time there was an unusual propaganda bonus.

Coinciding with the upcoming elections was the recent release of John Wayne's movie *The Green Berets*, a pro-war vanity piece for Wayne, hitting theaters across America in the summer of '68. It was unique in that it was the only new movie ever sent out to the A-teams.

Detachment A-231 had been running and re-running reels one, three and four of Charleton Heston's *The Agony and The Ecstacy*. Reel two had been damaged or lost. Montagnards really loved movies, any movie, especially cowboy movies. Movie night was a special occasion in camp, a big morale boost. Often the guys on the team would show the reels in any order or just two out of the three surviving reels since most movies didn't make any sense to the Yards anyway. Montagnards loved the "little dreams on the wall that could talk." They loved movies in color even better because McManus learned Montagnards always dreamt in color. When the team had the film *Waterhole Number Three* with James Coburn, they showed it five nights in a row.

The movie *The Green Berets* tied directly into North Vietnam's plans to manipulate the Presidential elections of 1968. A historical first, the North Vietnamese planned to use an American movie as reverse propaganda by overrunning and holding a camp against all odds. Weather would definitely be a factor in the enemy's favor. The Monsoon season in the central highlands had begun; bad weather was on its way.

McManus saw the movie. Like the others, it had been shown to the Yards on the Special Forces version of a drive-in movie. Instead of driving to the movie, the movie would drive to the audience. Ingeniously simple, a team member would put one of the camp's two small 10-kilowatt diesel generators in the back seat of a battered jeep, drive to an area of the camp and tack an old gray sheet to some trees. Nailing up the sheet signaled *Movie Tonight*. A buzz of excitement would sweep the camp. The Yards and their families would gather before dusk. No matter how many times they had seen a film, every night seemed like a premier. The team member running the show would put an old 16 mm projector on the hood of the jeep, plug it into the humming generator, and yell, "Camera, lights, action!" Magic took over the night. The Yards went wild.

But they panned *The Green Berets*! This came as a surprise for it was the only time they ever saw a movie that was about them. At first, the Yards cheered the actors in green berets but when they saw Vietnamese pretending to be Montagnards, they flipped out. It was a strong ethnic insult while some casting director in California may have thought it was a close match, the Yards were highly offended. In addition, the combat operations in the movie were farcical. The Montagnard strike force hooted and howled at the screen. To them, it was an action comedy. Nobody born in the jungle ever moved like that. The actors tip-toed about like a parody of Wiley Coyote sneaking up on the Road Runner. John Wayne had no clue.

McManus thought, sure, John Wayne loved the troops because he never had to be one of the troops. For weeks afterwards the Yards would point to a team member, hum the movie's theme song, and then fall down laughing hysterically.

McManus laughed also, but his laugh was hollow. He wanted so much for the movie to explain what they were up against. Like so many American soldiers in Vietnam, he was there in some ways because of movies he'd seen as a kid. Now he expected a movie to justify his war to its critics as if a movie could make it all right. *The Green Berets* was more than just a bad movie. It echoed the same romanticized war bullshit his uncles and their friends had spoon-fed McManus as a little kid. He saw his Montagnards as little guys thrown into a big meat grinder. Montagnard losses in these border operations weren't acknowledged in any way the American public would be aware of as they weren't really "on the books" or showing up even as Army of Vietnam statistics. Their losses didn't show up and yet were far heavier than those of their

American advisors both in absolute numbers and especially in relative terms, given the small size of even the largest tribes.

The Bourne Report, based on research compiled at several camps, concluded that men serving on A-teams in Vietnam in 1965 and 1966 had the highest mortality rate in *any* branch of the service, in *any* war, at *any* time. Factor in that McManus' team ran border ops in 1968. Almost thirty percent of all combat deaths during the entire ten years of the war occurred this one year. Think of what this means in terms of Montagnard losses. McManus wanted so much from Hollywood, and all he really got was Hollywood. The sizzle without the steak made him angry. Seeing his own war presented as a movie was a wake-up call for this dreamer. The movie tried to make them look good but failed miserably. The North Vietnamese were out to make them look bad before the Presidential election. From what he had seen so far, the NVA knew a hell of a lot more about war than John Fucking Wayne.

John Wayne and God

Rain fell. Angry monsoon rain. Wind-blasted rain pounded down in biblical floods. McManus felt lucky to be indoors, but guilty to be away from Tieu Atar when not out on an operation, if only for one night. He was sitting at the bar in the Moose's Lounge in Ban Me Thuot nursing a beer.

He'd come in for an A-Team Commanders' meeting and, like everybody in the bar who wasn't a member of the B-team, was stuck there that night because nothing could fly. They were all weathered-in. A grizzled sergeant who couldn't get a bird back up to Pleiku had just mentioned Ben Het. McManus overheard him talking.

"…So Mac was killed outright, but we know they took that Lieutenant alive."

McManus sidled up to the table, joining the listeners. "This Lieutenant, know anything about him?" He asked.

The sergeant looked at McManus over the top of his beer can, sizing him up. "Not much, he was a *newby*." Only in the camp little over a few months. Hadn't been in country long but he fit in. Heard the guys liked him." He looked off into memory, "Damn shame about Mac. Good man. Third tour. Good in the woods."

McManus took a long drink of beer. He cleared his throat, voice strained, "Know his name?"

The sergeant lit an unfiltered cigarette. Took a few seconds. He spit a flake of tobacco from his lip, screwing up his face in thought.

"Name began with an 'L,' it'll come to me, 'L' something, something like that."

"Maybe Leonard?" McManus asked.

"Yeah, yeah, that's it! Leonard, y'know him?"

McManus didn't answer. His mind was already off somewhere else, screaming at God. John Wayne and God. He's pissed at both of them.

More Than Just A Little Bit

August rolled in on tropical lightning. The normally bad weather became outrageously unpredictable. Everything got progressively worse. Tieu Atar's small laterite and clay-mix airstrip began to wash away in torrents of rain. Planes couldn't land. Helicopters flew at risk, if at all. The team house, where most of them slept, flooded with a foot of water. Enemy activity in the area increased threefold. A rat bit the medic.

A Montagnard had a bad dream about August 5th. A huddle of somber Yards brought the dream to McManus just after noon on the 4th. They wanted him to know, to prepare. It took a while to understand. The operation scheduled to go out early next morning would get into a big firefight as soon as they moved off of the helicopter landing zone. The dreamer feared he'd be shot as they made contact. McManus listened pensively, then counseled him not to be afraid. The man shouldn't put any faith in bad dreams. While he didn't mean it quite the way it came out, the Yards understood McManus to be telling the man his dream was caused

by something he ate. The dreamer shook his head sadly. He said
something in the Rhade language that McManus couldn't follow.
The Yard looked at him as though he were too much beaucoup
crazy. He sighed, exasperated. McManus mistook his last few
words to mean *What's the use*.

Early the next morning in a morning fog the helicopters lifted off.
Ten minutes after the first insertion a major firefight erupted. The
Montagnard who had brought McManus his dream took a nasty
wound, high on the thigh, and disappeared into chest-high
elephant grass. Sergeant First Class Joe Lopez, the team's heavy
weapons specialist, found him, unconscious but alive. He had lost
a lot of blood. Lopez threw him on a helicopter shuttling more
troops and ammo into the battle, which flew him back to camp for
triage. The bullet missed the bone but did serious muscle damage.
Tyre, the medic on-site, treated the wound, stabilizing the injured
dreamer while Wiley tried to rustle up a medivac to shuttle him
to the hospital up in Pleiku. Request went out *Critical Soonest*.

As dusk darkened the mist, McManus waited with the wounded
at the edge of their eroding airstrip. A gentle rain fell out of the
thickening fog.

Distant explosions and thunder rolled out of the night. If the
medivac couldn't see the strobe light when McManus flashed it,
the wounded wouldn't get out. If the man spent the night, he
would die. Special Forces Medics were the brightest and most
highly motivated men McManus had ever known. Russ Tyre was
one of the best but, as good as Tyre was, he didn't have the
medical equipment or backup to keep this Yard alive. The

dreamer lay on a stretcher, and though sedated, spoke quietly to Whet, a Montagnard interpreter who leaned over him. McManus heard the helicopter and signaled once, twice, and the medivac acknowledged them, circling in. Only on the helipad for a minute, the chopper took on the injured men and lifted up into the night fog. McManus felt some relief but also a greater sense of failure. He had been warned the landing zone would be hot. McManus had chosen to not listen to the Montagnard dreamer. He had planned this operation. He'd received an occult form of intelligence from this man and ignored it for what it really was. McManus had sent them into an ambush because he was a know-it-all smart-ass American who was afraid to believe in their dreams because of his own dream.

He asked Whet about an expression the wounded man had used.

He'd heard similar words when they first discussed the dream the day before. The man had repeated them as they waited for the "dust-off." McManus didn't understand the Montagnard's words either time.

Whet hedged a bit, but when pressed, told him in mangled English, "Too many much time in dream talk, you too big asshole."

McManus was startled, maybe even hurt. Whet tried to soften his words.

In a gentle voice, he added, "We love you too much, you too much have good man's heart."

The hard rain started again. The sound of the helicopter disappeared into the growing darkness. The chopper's familiar whump-whumping faded into distant sounds of war and thunder. McManus stared at the spot where the med-e-vac disappeared in the night. He thought of the Montagnard's dream, what it meant for his own haunting dream. More than ever he felt like a doomed man. A frighteningly violent flash of light punctuated the moment. The lightning struck nearby, less than a quarter mile away. Startled, McManus and Whet jumped. Whet laughed nervously. Staggering on shaky legs, McManus couldn't see. He shuddered. In the dark after the flash, McManus stood alone in his world of confusion. He tried to remember who said, "Humankind cannot bear very much reality." The answer didn't come to him. He knew one thing though; he knew whatever his fate would be, it wasn't something subtle sneaking up on him. In total blackness, he heard thunder rumble in heavy rolls like great guns and angry gods.

Fat Tuesday

Unconfirmed reports filtered down through intelligence sources about the missing lieutenant from Ben Het. McManus now understood the man was Leonard. An across-the-border "asset" had seen a captured American answering Leonard's description. Badly hurt, not doing well, they were keeping him alive, slowly moving him north up the Ho Chi Minh trail.

Intelligence couldn't get a good fix on a location. "Mad Dog" Schriver and "Baby San" Davidson had been sent to look for him. There wasn't a better pair in Special Ops. They couldn't get a fix on him. The enemy moved Leonard often. His prospects didn't look good. McManus felt sick with guilt every time he heard any mention of him. Had he not met Sutton that first day in Nha Trang this could be him. He was glad the enemy was keeping Leonard alive.

It didn't seem possible, but things seemed to keep getting worse for his fears about the 17th. A North Vietnamese Colonel captured near Pleiku reinforced prevailing intelligence theories. The Intelligence Section wasn't certain if he was lying very well or really willing to cooperate but either way, his song was a sad one for McManus. A major offensive would be launched against a Special Forces border camp, but the prisoner added, specifically, the attack would come just after the 15th of August. "All Americans in the camp must die!" he had said emphatically. No matter what the cost, the North Vietnamese were ordered to overrun and hold the camp for at least three days. Modern war plays to the media. The enemy's sacrifice must last long enough for news media to create a major story. The message meant to shock America, to demonstrate the enemy could overwhelm a Green Beret Camp anytime they wanted. McManus and the sergeant in the commo shed reading the top secret message looked at each other. McManus said, "Who didn't know that?" Wiley's answer seemed to come through a ring of his cigar smoke, "Big fucking deal."

Wiley re-read the encrypted message he had deciphered on the one time pad. He made a face, "This team goes to bed every night knowing if these little bastards want to throw enough men on our wire they can be eating our corn flakes for breakfast. The best we can do is make them pay." McManus took the message from Wiley and read to himself. "This NVA colonel keeps saying the same thing, No matter what the cost, they intend to take and hold a border camp for at least three days. This rings true. I think they can certainly take a camp... but three days?" The thought hung in the air. They both knew a reaction force could retake the camp and if everyone were either dead or had slipped through the wire into the jungle, the B-52s would come in and flatten everything.

Not much of a consolation prize if it's your camp. McManus handed the one-time pad back to Wiley. "The damage to the reputation of Special Forces in the minds of the American voters who support the war would justify the severe price the NVA would certainly have to pay. I think this guy's the real deal." Wiley agreed.

The following day Wiley brought McManus another top secret message from intelligence further supporting what the NVA Colonel said. It revealed the communications headquarters for the First North Vietnamese Army Division had relocated their radio base from a sanctuary in Cambodia, directly west of Pleiku, to the southern side of Chu Pong Mountain across the border in Cambodia. A major move, over 80 kilometers south, this put them in an area known as "The Wasteland" because it was considered inhospitable. There wasn't as much water in the area and thus not as much wildlife. NVA units moving south on "The Trail" preferred to move through it as quickly as possible. The mid-point of this area was directly across the border from Tieu Atar exactly where the NVA radio signals now originated.

The North Vietnamese Army Headquarters Communications Center had been operating directly west of Pleiku since early 1964. This relocation was a major development. McManus studied the message, and the two men agreed this was a strong indication of trouble coming their way. Of all the A-Teams situated close to the border, A-231 was the least prepared to defend itself since the engineers had been nervous working so close to the Ia Drang Valley, bailing out before completing the camp.

The team spent their spare time cutting down trees to clear better fields of fire. They still didn't have clear fields of fire on all sides of the camp in some areas, and the jungle growth came almost right up to the outer wire. A-231 set records burning up chain saws. Supply-type efficiency experts back at headquarters accused the team of misusing the saws and refused to issue any more. A new guy on the team, Carter, one of the team's two combat engineers and demolitions men had to be restrained. He wanted to go down to Nha Trang with the team's last saw and cut the paper pusher's desk in half.

Didn't matter anyway. The team couldn't make the camp defensible in time if they had an army of engineers with bulldozers. Large trees loomed over the inner perimeter. In principles of defense, this was insanity. The trees would cause air bursts from incoming mortar rounds making even a miss or near hit much more effective. In essence, Tieu Atar was indefensible. The North Vietnamese knew it. The team knew it. To their credit, they went out and worked improving camp defenses every day they weren't out running operations trying to find the enemy. The workload was both intensely exhausting inside the wire and very dangerous outside the wire. To a man, aggressively overconfident, they much preferred to be outside the camp taking the war to the enemy rather than waiting for the enemy to come to them. McManus stood on top of a sandbagged bunker and looked out at the encroaching jungle. He frowned, thinking *John Wayne you can kiss my rosy-red Irish ass.*

Bad weather didn't stop them or even slow them down. The team chopped trees furiously all day long even in the heaviest rain. One tree fell the full length of McManus' last operational three quarter ton truck, crushing it into the mud. He heard the crash and ran out of the team house to see what happened, looking at what moments before had been his last usable vehicle. He looked at Tyre and Hank who were both covered in mud. Tyre had been supervising the tree cutting detail. Hank ran out as soon as he heard the crash. Wearing flip flops, he slipped losing one. He was pissed and ready for a fight. Tyre, pleading his case in this fuckup, getting nowhere.

McManus screamed at both of them. "I had to sign for this useless piece of shit! My name's on the property books. They could take this out of my pay!" He couldn't even say it with a straight face. It symbolized what he was beginning to feel about the war; a sad combination of bad luck and stupidity. The team started laughing at him. Lopez said he had an expression on his face like Wiley Coyote in a Roadrunner cartoon. That's just great. The coyote image again, just like the clowns in John Wayne's movie. McManus had grown up loving war movies, the fuel of his imagination as a kid. Americans always kicked ass, always came out on top. McManus' war was now morphing into a fucking Roadrunner cartoon.

With the coyote's bemused expression on his face, he stood admitting to himself fully, for the very first time with no reservations, that on August 17th some very major shit-storm was coming at him.

Couldn't duck it.

No way out.

No off button.

No escape.

August 17th, was coming on like a storm, so were the North Vietnamese.

All his childhood fantasies leading to this moment in the mud were gone. McManus' war wasn't a movie. No rehearsals or retakes, his only script a dream he couldn't comprehend. Mired in mud, he stood there, his only defense a wry grin. The men on his team laughed at him as he screamed, his face turned up at the raining sky, "Mardi Gras! I can't believe I thought this would be a fucking Mardi Gras!"

Farewell To Arms

Rain poured down in torrents. Thirty-something inches in three days hammering the tin roof of the team house like a drunken troop of monkeys wielding ball-peen hammers. An overwhelming incredible sound. Water, the color of black coffee, flooded the floor eight inches deep. Men sloshed around in flip flops and rolled up pants. They made do with it, kept their sense of humor, and built rickety little boardwalks with scrap lumber. Nobody complained. It was simply life on the border. A cardboard sign read "Welcome to Atlantic City." The team balanced on the boards precariously as if they were part of a high wire act. For McManus they were.

At night he dreamed the dream, always in color. It was the color that confused him. He awoke with a clear image of what *day* the dream was about, but the action of the dream was lost in a mist of many colors. All he could be sure of, something was coming on like the monsoon rains beating like war drums on the leaking roof. The sound in the dream was a stunning, incoherent, overwhelming roar. A scream, but not only one voice. In the dramatic mist or colored fog, he had no idea who or what made this incredible noise. Almost human, it was a sound unlike anything he'd ever heard.

McManus woke up on his back, soaking wet. Water, as if from a hose, streamed in on him from a hole in the roof. A box floated by with a live rat in it. It made him smile as his world might be rotting away, but his sense of the absurd was still intact. He sat up saying, "God, you don't have to piss directly on me." Hank, the acting team sergeant, an old border runner who had pulled several operations along the "red line" with McManus, laughed hysterically from the lower bunk. Hank laughed so hard he could barely speak, "You don't know how funny you are, man." McManus, afraid of himself, thought Hank had no idea how funny he was getting. It was a long time before he trusted himself enough to get back to sleep. Something about Hank's name was eerily familiar in a way that haunted him.

And then it came to him. He knew the name from something he'd read in school. He smiled in the dark. Hank's last name was Henry. He went by Hank or Henry. Nobody called him Fred. McManus lay in the dark waiting for sleep to take him back to tortured dreams, mulling over the notion the man he ran border operations with had the same name as Hemingway's anti-hero in *A Farewell To Arms*. Frederick Henry. He wondered if there was some farewell to arms in his future, his mind adrift in that mist of many colors.

A Dark Grey Curtain

On the morning of August 16th   McManus sloshed out of camp with Hank and seventy-two Montagnards. Dolly, a sixteen-year-old Montagnard, was commander of the Yards and Whet, another Montagnard who spoke some English, but not very well, was their interpreter. Over a few beers the night before, while poring over maps and kicking around ideas, McManus had given Dolly the M-16 an engineer had left behind. He was the only Yard to have one, and he was on top of the world. Giving Dolly an M-16, a big deal.

On this operation, McManus felt as if he carried the weight of his whole life in his rucksack, every thought, experience and sin on his back. They were heading out to the Cambodian border. If something was coming for him on the 17th, he couldn't sit in camp and wait for it. He would go out to meet it. Hank, emaciated from two back-to-back tours "in country," was almost six feet tall, and walked just behind the point element. He turned before disappearing into the mist and smiled, his big grin standing out against a dark stubble of beard. In his faded tiger-stripe fatigues, Hank seemed to melt into the green-wet day, almost disappearing bit by bit as he moved through an opening in the tangles of barbed wire. Hank was there, but he wasn't there, as though only part of him could be seen when he stood still. The Yards loved Hank and treated him with a sense of awe. So did McManus. Hank taught him a lot about combat patrolling in the jungle.

McManus knew he was fortunate to run with Hank, Dolly, and Whet. They'd run operations several times now and had an easy feeling for each other as a team, a strong intuitive feeling of where they'd all be, what they'd do when gunfire ripped air.

The weather turned pure monsoon. The strike force was definitely going out in the enemy's favorite time of year. If they ran into the NVA, the enemy would have an overwhelming advantage in firepower. Forget air support, it wouldn't be a factor. Probably couldn't muster up even a medivac or resupply chopper in an emergency. They would be on their own. The current storm front was predicted to hold up for at least several days.

Artillery support was something else they wouldn't have. Regular American units never ventured outside their bases without it. If they moved from their base, Chinooks and skyhook helicopters brought artillery with them. They would plot a fan shape on the map and only move within the fan shaped area covered by artillery. If the operation had to go farther, they'd bring in another firebase first, then configure a new fan to keep them covered. Wherever the American line units went, they almost always had cannon fire covering the terrain. Even in bad weather, accurate artillery fire was available moments after contact with the enemy.

The strike force moved too far and too fast for artillery. They wouldn't have access to artillery no matter what. They would act as a guerilla force using speed and surprise against the NVA the way the Viet Cong had done to American units. Hank and the team had an "attitude." They were arrogant, but the lack of air support due to the weather front gnawed at McManus. Shaping up as a big mismatch, if not for his dream McManus would have liked to sit this out in camp. But he had this nagging fear that staying in camp might draw more of his people into danger. He felt he had few options and a growing feeling that his mystical test wasn't going to be any kind of a multiple choice.

Moving through the jungle in torrential rainfall was both exhausting and dangerous. Bad as a night movement but more miserable, wearing you down with a draining fatigue. McManus tasted an acidic fear in his mouth. They stopped to rest and eat just after noon, less than eight kilometers southwest of camp. The day was harsh, dark gray, almost no visibility. They were making good time, considering the conditions, maybe great time. It wasn't a concern. They had a general direction for the patrol and an area near the border they wanted to check out but no real destination. Their goal wasn't so much a specific place but an event. Once they got close to the "red line" they'd move parallel to the border looking for an enemy trail then set up ambushes. They would hunker down in the jungle and wait. And wait.

Hank came up to McManus, water running off the tip of his nose. He squinted at his watch in disgust. Only two feet from McManus he had to shout to be heard above the sound of rain.

"Just fuckin' great! High fuckin' noon and it's so fuckin' dark I can't see twenty feet! Thank God there's no fuckin' mist!"

How like Hank to thank God and curse in the same breath. McManus should have kept his mouth shut but didn't. "Gonna be a heavy mist tomorrow, Hank. Had a dream about it." As he spoke, Hank had already turned to move away. He stopped, grabbed McManus' arm firmly, leaning in close to him. McManus could smell his terrible breath, he'd been eating the foul fermented fish sauce the Yards ate. "You can take this Montagnard shit too fuckin' far, y' know," Hank looked genuinely concerned. Running border operations along the red line was walking on serious ground and running them with a crazy partner didn't cut the odds in your favor.

"A heavy mist tomorrow, Hank. And colors. It was in my dream." McManus went further out on the limb. Something he started to sense.

"We'll be all right, you'll see." For McManus, it was the first time since the incident in the book store that he felt any comfort with his premonition. It was the first time he had ever shared any of this with another. For Hank, it was something different.

Hank gave him a funny look, squinting, a smile in his eyes, wary yet amused, water still dripping off his nose. He laughed, lowered his head looking at the ground, shook his head slowly from side to side, muttered, "Colors" in a little chuckle and walked away. The rain fell behind him like a dark gray curtain.

The Hazard of the Die

On the evening of the 16th, their first day out, the operation moved through dense jungle heading generally west-southwest. McManus noted the Yards were spooked. A light mist formed. Something was in the air. A tiger followed them, they kept hearing it, out there in the haze somewhere. The jungle hiding something you could sense but not see.

As visibility started to fade, they came across a fresh enemy trail. Someone had been through here recently, coming in from Cambodia. He knew if they followed it west it would link up with the Ho Chi Minh trail. They weren't up for that, given the lack of air support. They had to be patient and only take on an enemy they could overwhelm then get out of the area. In this weather, they had to hoard every slight advantage, be stationary, prepared, quiet, focused. Had to hit first, keep them off balance, hold the momentum, and if you lose it, then run like hell, drawing them into hastily laid ambushes and booby traps.

John McManus and Fred Henry ran effective operations. They never used enemy trails no matter how inviting. In this low visibility, it would be suicidal. First, they moved their men backward, away from the trail, creating their own trail parallel to the enemy's but not too close, advancing extremely slowly and quietly towards the border until they found an optimal site for an ambush. Then they would crawl into position inching closer to the enemy trail. With seventy-six men, to maintain noise and movement discipline, they would move only a few hundred yards, at most. If it took them hours to do this, they would consider it time well-invested in security and surprise. They would leave no sign on the enemy trail that anyone was in the area.

McManus and Hank decided to set up several large ambushes along the trail and settle in for the night. They would also set up an ambush behind them should the enemy try to roll up their flanks and encircle them once they made contact. The terrain they chose would make the enemy react in certain logical ways that would work to the strike force's advantage. This wasn't their first dance. They established radio contact with Tieu Atar, reported their *Remain Over Night* location or "RON" via a coded message and let them know they'd found a large trail. Then they imposed strict radio silence. McManus, over twelve miles from camp and much closer to the Cambodian Border, might just "lay doggo" tomorrow and see what would walk into the ambush.

Tomorrow would be the 17th. Here he was, settling in for the night in an ambush on a very large enemy trail. McManus felt a little giddy. Definitely rolling the dice, he sat wrapped in his poncho. A line from *Richard The Third*, a thought before battle, crossed his mind. He contemplated the words to himself as if a prayer:

I have set my life upon a cast, and I will stand the hazard of the die.

Something was going to happen. McManus had little hope it could be anything good. As he prepared to go to sleep in the jungle, the rain fell and the night came down to wrap itself around him like a heavy cloak woven from his sins and his fears.

A Good and
Unexpected Sign

It rained all through the night. McManus awoke thinking he was in his dream. An exceptionally light rain, mixed with a heavy fog, filtered through the jungle. Everything he looked at had a strangely opaque glow. He felt as though he was looking at his life through frosted glass. He didn't want a clearer picture. He didn't really want to see everything. Hank watched him closely as if something he didn't want to believe was beginning to dawn on him. McManus hoped Hank wouldn't get mangled on this day. He didn't know if he'd done the right thing bringing him along. He wasn't sure about a lot of things anymore.

Rolling out of his jungle hammock he began to heat water in a small tin C-ration can, a little green can that had once held peaches. He created fire using a small piece of plastique explosive. Burning it made an odorless, smokeless flame. He pushed the heel of his boot into the soft ground and lit the explosive, dropping it into the hole he made. The little flame was so small it couldn't be seen from even two feet away as it heated the coffee. McManus wanted the pleasure of a morning cup of coffee and a quiet moment. He would be having a battered can of terrible instant coffee, but he was okay with that.

Today was August 17th, 1968, and he felt a strange sense of being where he should be. McManus felt content. Content was okay. He was going to enjoy his coffee and take the day as it came. Squatting like a Montagnard, stirring his coffee with a little stick, McManus heard his operational code name come out of the radio a few feet away. He recognized the voice. He didn't expect to hear it this morning on the back side of this incredible weather front.

"Bat Guano, Bat Guano, This is Pterodactyl Three Five, over."

Happy to hear Three Five's voice, McManus picked up the radio handset and answered his friend, Bob Shryock, a pilot, flying somewhere near them in a light observation plane known as a Bird Dog.

"Three Five this is Bat Guano. Read you 'five by,' how me? Over."

McManus had acknowledged Three Five's transmission and told him he could hear him loud and clear, "five by five" was radioman slang from old Morse code procedures, shorthand for as *loud* and as *clear* as possible. He asked how well Three Five could read his transmission.

"Bat Guano, Three Five. Have you 'five by' also. Drop ten, out."

The "drop ten" was a personal code of opposites they had established between them so they could talk freely without some staff officer back in Ban Me Thuot horning in. Everything they said to each other at the opening meant the opposite and double the number. When Three Five told Bat Guano to *Drop Ten* he actually meant to go *Up Twenty* clicks on the radio frequency. McManus said, "Roger, out" adjusting his radio quickly to the new channel 20 clicks higher. The more powerful radios at higher headquarters would lose their transmission.

"Bee Gee this is Five over."

"Five, Gee here, go." Pterodactyl Three Five continued in a casual drawl, just a guy at work. "There's a nasty weather front. Slipped out of 'Toot' (Ban Me Thuot) before dawn and flew up the back side of the red line to get around it. Used up a lot of fuel buckin' headwinds. I'll head to your house and save fuel till you need me. Think the boys can rustle up some 'grease' for me? Missed breakfast, over."

From what McManus knew of the weather front, Three Five had to have taken off early, gone down below Duc Lap two camps south of Tieu Atar, then crossed into Cambodian airspace illegally to end up over him by flying north on the Cambodian side of the border west of the storm, crossing back just across from Tieu Atar.

This was much more than just risky business. Three Five would have had to file a false pre-flight plan and then violate international law and every military prohibition and order involving flying within five kilometers of the Border. He risked big trouble if the authorities got wind of this and even greater risk if the enemy got hold of him. Three Five was an unsung hero; he did whatever it took to help the guys on the ground. McManus was glad to have him up there, especially this day. Without a drastic change in weather, no planes would make it here from Ban Me Thuot through the storm. McManus had eyes in the sky now. Three Five had gone to a lot of risk and trouble.

For McManus and Hank, this was a big break. If they ran into something Three Five could get back down here and give them an eagle's eye view, weather permitting. If Three Five had crashed anywhere over in Cambodia the enemy's trail watchers would have boiled him alive.

It was a good and unexpected sign to have Three Five in the area.

A Ticket to the Big Dance

Stirring sugar and powdered milk into his coffee, McManus looked up and saw Whet herding a somber group of Yards into the clearing between him and Hank, who watched them warily not twenty feet away. McManus knew Hank would be annoyed these men had left their ambush positions. Montagnards are delightfully pleasant people, but no one in this party smiled. They were beaucoup very serious. Without anyone saying anything, they circled McManus, squatting down around his heating coffee.

Whet didn't make eye contact when he spoke, "Bat Guano, this man has much terrible, many bad time dream." McManus listened and played that sentence again in his head. Gotta love the words. Whet had reached deep within himself to find these words. McManus marveled at what they were trying to say. Whet's face was troubled. McManus knew these mangled English French words were only half of Whet's communication problem. The other half, the real challenge, simply getting McManus to listen. Whet needn't have worried.

A frightened Montagnard repeatedly nodded as Whet told McManus of images from the night. The dream foretold a "Much beaucoup many big fight and too much men die." Whet repeated the words "Too much men die," as the man who had the dream nodded emphatically understanding the words in some universal way, not what they meant but in how Whet said them. As Whet tried to explain, the Yards standing around him were clearly upset by this dream. The boy who had the dream would often interrupt, adding something in Rhade he wanted Whet to tell McManus, nodding again as he listened. They were scared. McManus had never seen them this way. They were scaring him. Through a gap in the small circle, across the clearing at the edge of the mist, he could see Hank listening. Hank's eyes, large and white, watched warily. McManus listened and asked no questions until they were finished. McManus, looking directly into the eyes of the little dreamer, spoke respectfully, "This is a very serious dream."

Everyone looked at him. He told them in a calm voice that this dream was doubly serious because he had also been having a dream about this very day for a beaucoup long time, even before he came to their mountains from far away America. Their eyes grew larger as Whet attempted to translate McManus' words into Rhade. Whet's grasp of English was so poor McManus couldn't be sure what he was telling the Yards, but from the look on their faces, something was getting through. He turned and looked at Hank whose mouth hung open, a great gaping "O." McManus thought Hank looked like a fish.

McManus revealed another part of the dream. It was true there would be a big battle. He emphasized his dream revealed none of the Montagnards were in any danger. None of them would come to harm. McManus said, "This battle is to test me, not you." McManus spoke his truth. Truth has a ring to it. They all knew McManus spoke from his heart. McManus revealed his challenge was somewhere in a mist of many colors. He wasn't thinking this out or planning ahead what to say. As he spoke, he heard his thoughts in the exact moment others heard them. They came as much a revelation to him as to everyone else.

"If I meet the test we're all safe. If I fail, if someone must die, it's me. This dream is why I am here." McManus felt his burden lift and fly away. The circle of Montagnards looked at McManus with complete shock. Montagnards don't hide their feelings. They don't even understand why anyone should. They have little guile. Sadness came into their eyes. McManus' soldiers seemed to be mourning him already. He said it again slowly, adding, "It's going to be okay." Whet interpreted words the men already seemed to comprehend. Whet seemed relieved. McManus asked Whet to teach him words in Rhade to say *It will be okay; it is all going to be okay.* McManus listened carefully, then repeated the words to the group several times, smiling calmly, making eye contact with each man in the circle. They nodded to him. He told Whet to tell them in this battle they would be great heroic soldiers. McManus' magic on this day was going to be very great, very strong, *Many Beaucoup Magics.*

McManus didn't know why he was so calm or why he told them what he did. He didn't know where his words came from. He just knew they were true. McManus felt this was all part of a dream he had lived many times. He had somehow known these words before as though remembering a piece of a dream that he had forgotten.

The Montagnards were completely satisfied. In their mystical world of dreams, this all made sense.

They stared at Bat Guano.

There was nothing more to say.

They took one final look at him as though it was both the first time they had ever seen him and maybe also their last. They thanked him politely and moved away to spread the good word.

The Great Oz had spoken.

As the Montagnards disappeared into the mist at the edge of the small clearing, he could hear the little Montagnard who had brought him his dream, repeating McManus' expression *many beaucoup magics*, the Yard's awkward pronunciation trailing into a sweet little giggle of relief. Another soft Montagnard voice repeated, in their primal language, McManus' expression, *It will be okay*. McManus felt his dream speaking. Fading into the fog, the small, dark men disappeared.

He felt calm but didn't know why. Almost as a release, an inappropriate small laugh escaped from him as he once again realized Whet didn't know "Bat Guano" was his radio call sign, not his real name. Nor did Whet know it meant "bat shit." He sat stirring his coffee, that Wiley Coyote-look on his face when he caught Henry watching him, slowly shaking his head. He laughed as he started to say something about "Bat Guano's Modern Montagnard Management program" when a voice came out of the radio.

"Bat Guano, Bat Guano, this is Three Five, over."

Taking the radio handset, McManus acknowledged the call and waited for Three Five to continue.

"Want to go into harm's way Bat Guano? Found what looks to be big doings, northwest a bit. Wanna ticket to the big dance? Over."

Three Five had found something between McManus and the camp, something McManus couldn't ignore. He stood up. His can of coffee was lying on its side. He stood in a small puddle of what had been his coffee. He'd kicked it over when he reached for the radio. August 17th, here we go, here we go.

Pterodactyl Three Five told McManus that heading north to the camp he'd played a hunch and worked his way west towards the border. He'd found an unbelievably fresh trail. Whatever made the trail was large and holed up while he was circling the jungle canopy that hid them. He flew east towards the camp and thought he could tell where they were headed next. Have to be an area large enough to give good overhead cover and adequate water. Something outrageous was moving due East. The trail leading into a jungle area Three Five felt they were holed up in was so large and fresh he could almost guarantee where this dragon's next lair would be, where they must be headed next. All McManus had to do, on his long awaited August the 17th, get there first. Three Five kept saying "It's gonna be big. It's gonna be big." McManus was looking across the clearing at Hank, monitoring the same message on the other radio, the mist getting thicker. He couldn't see Hank as clearly as he could have, what seemed lifetimes ago when he started heating water for coffee. He noticed Whet moving around the perimeter whispering encouragement to the Yards, Whet never taking his eyes off him. Hank gave the signal to "saddle up." As they prepared to roll, the mist thickened, the rain becoming a steady drizzle. McManus grinned.

Hank, an unlit cigarette in his mouth, gave McManus *the finger*.

Let It Happen

Shortly before seven a.m., they rolled out, their formation in three columns, with the two much smaller flanking columns to protect the main body from walking into an ambush. First they headed north, then veered west towards Cambodia. McManus wanted to set up an ambush near the stream junction Pterodactyl Three Five was fairly certain might be home to an enemy base camp. This would position his Montagnard strike force between the enemy and Tieu Atar. No matter how carefully they moved, large units leave a trail in elephant grass. In the rainy season, the jungle would repair itself in a few days. As long as the small plane circled the area in which he thought they were right now, the enemy would stay hidden. Three Five could tell where the enemy had stopped and probably where they were headed. This wasn't Three Five's first dance either.

McManus and Hank wanted to beat the enemy unit to their probable base camp, the stream junction affording great overhead cover. It was turning into a race. Three Five couldn't hold the enemy in place for long, his fuel critical. To save fuel, Three Five headed up to their camp. He planned to get something to eat and monitor the operation on the radio while sitting at the picnic table in the team house.

He'd be sitting in his plane ready to crank it up around eleven or as soon as McManus called for backup. Three Five had circled as long as he could over where he thought the enemy unit was hiding, and barring something unforeseen, McManus thought he could get to their base camp ahead of them and set up a reception committee. It was a cross country race through the jungle. Now, settled in the team house at Tieu Atar, Three Five was teasing McManus. He asked how they could live the way they did. Three Five sounded like a little kid. He'd never seen so many rats, snakes or so much water and muddy slime indoors. Fliers weren't used to substandard housing.

They arrived at the stream junction about twenty after eleven. There were two large trails generally heading southeast but a week old. Another operation from Tieu Atar had a firefight south of the camp last week, probably with a unit that made one of these trails. No fresh trails led into the stream junction. Hank told Three Five to stay on the ground while they scouted it out. "If we stir something up, we'll call you," Hank told him. McManus and Hank established several interlocking ambushes on the approach from Cambodia. If an enemy unit tried to outflank their ambush they'd bump into another one. Hank and McManus formed tight, mutually supporting, blocking forces in case the enemy broke away. Economy of Force, one of the Principles of War, something Hank had mastered. He could position a small force more effectively than anyone McManus had ever known, with the possible exception of Janus Rozanski. Hank, Whet, and several Yards from "recon squad" slipped into the stream. Low in the water, they moved upstream into the enemy base camp to snoop around. McManus waited.

He could feel his heart throbbing. He didn't like being without an interpreter if something happened to them. It was a calculated risk that could morph into a colossal fuck-up, but Hank needed Whet with him at the moment. The wait seemed forever. In a little over half an hour, Hank came out of the stream and crawled next to McManus shaking his head ominously. "It's a battalion or larger base camp, more of a way station. This is an overnight stop for the big boys, the really big boys." Given the size of the Montagnard strike force they were leading, McManus and Hank were way out of their class, off the scale out of their class.

Hank said, "This place is really decked out." He thought a minute. "Empty now, won't be for long." McManus nodded. "Somebody laid out a lot of fresh fruit, rice, and even fish." He spoke in an offhand manner, unconcerned as if this had nothing to do with him. Hank bit down on a juicy *Cam*, kind of like an orange. "Hey, this is really good!" He offered McManus a bite. McManus shook his head No.

Rainfall doubled in intensity. They were kneeling in muddy water. Water ran everywhere, as though a dam had broken.

Time on their side, they moved some ambushes around, several right into the base camp, setting them up on the most likely avenues of approach. A chess game, with Hank as the Grand

Master, maximizing the little he had, tweaking every possible advantage. McManus established a tiny perimeter on a low hill where he could best control or defend the area if they had to fall back. It was also the best spot for the strongest radio signal to the A-team. Prepared if something happened, with good radio communications to the only help they could hope for, he let the team know their exact location and what they had found. With their stronger radios, the team passed this information on to higher headquarters in Ban Me Thuot. "Higher" said they probably couldn't do anything with air cover in case McManus got into trouble. Pterodactyl Three Five relayed this from the radio in his plane sitting on the runway at Tieu Atar. "Nothing can fly right now; nothing we have can get through the storm front between Ban Me Thuot and the border." Static crackled out of the handset. Three Five came on again, "Ban Me Thuot says you're probably on your own. They said good luck." Hank smiled, "Tell them to go fuck themselves!" Three Five's laughter crackled out of the radio.

McManus and Hank sat in the enemy base camp waiting like Goldilocks in the nursery rhyme for the three bears to come home, tired, hungry and cranky. The Montagnards were getting cozy after eating the food they had found and thought they could take a nap in the missing bears' little beds. Hank wasn't gonna let that happen. This was no fairy tale. McManus was neither sleepy nor hungry. Strangely enough, August 17th didn't cross his mind.

Chalky mists moved over them in sometimes thick, sometimes thin patches. One minute they could see for twenty-five or thirty yards, the next they couldn't see ten feet. Hank had just come back from making the rounds, checking out his ambush positions, making sure some of the Montagnards stayed awake. McManus stood near Hank and Whet. Hank said, "Something is not right, your great heroic soldiers are all awake. They smell this thing coming." As soon as he spoke, a frenetic Montagnard ran up to Whet.

Within seconds another Yard came out of the haze and interrupted the first man trying to speak. As the two Yards competed for Whet's attention, interrupting each other, a third, then fourth, and finally a fifth Montagnard ran out of the mist, obviously telling Whet things were getting worse. Each arriving Yard brought newer "intel" of more columns of the enemy. A sixth Yard ran up with the latest news flash. They all turned to him for the update. Hank's question "Who's left in my ambush?" went unanswered. Comically animated but not funny, the Yards were deadly serious. You didn't have to speak their language to know the wheels were coming off the wagon.

When Hank and McManus got through to Whet, the gist of the panic seemed to be the first Yard was saying some VC, Viet Cong, were approaching their ambush. Each subsequent Yard said more, then even beaucoup many more, columns were approaching from the west in different sightings. To Yards, all enemy are labeled VC, even NVA soldiers in full uniform. One or two Yards confirmed these "VC" were fully outfitted, uniformed soldiers. These guys weren't rag tag Viet Cong. These guys were hard core North Vietnamese Army Regulars with all the organization, weapons and tactics that came with it.

The first Yard said a point element of NVA scouts had pulled up at the far edge of a large clearing, across from one of the ambush sites, and stopped.

That was enough for Hank, who took one man by the scruff of the neck and headed down there to see for himself. "Get Three Five on the horn," he said over his shoulder. McManus had already alerted Tieu Atar while he tried to sort it out. The Yards were acting like there were thousands of them. Montagnards have no written language and don't have many words for numbers. Most Yards can't count well. Those who can, can't count very high and McManus knew even his interpreters were sketchy with large numbers. Amounts well above what you could count on your fingers were all labeled some version of "many." The Yards jumping up and down in front of McManus and Whet conveyed they were overwhelmingly outnumbered and their dicks were in the dirt. Precise numbers didn't matter. The final consensus: "Beaucoup too many numbah ten VC fuck!" meant big trouble.

McManus got on the radio, as Three Five cranked up his plane. The mist was lifting, ground visibility sometimes up to fifty or sixty feet. Across from the ambush site, less than a football field away, the point elements of seven large columns of men, maybe a thousand to twelve hundred men, were waiting for the base camp to be checked out by their point recon. The first men the NVA would send in were usually the best men they had from one of their elite hunter-killer teams that took the point and rear guard when they were moving through the jungle. Three columns moving into a base camp would normally indicate a company sized unit. Five Columns coming in meant a battalion, but seven columns on the move, multiple battalions!

Both sides knew something was wrong. Base camps always had a trail watcher stationed there all the time to prevent situations like this and to escort a unit into camp. The trail watcher would be the one who put out the fresh fruit, fish, and rice. Where was he? He had screwed up big-time and would really suffer for a mistake of this caliber, but that would come later. Right now both sides knew the other was there, but neither side knew exactly what they were up against. The small advantage of any surprise McManus and Hank might have had was gone.

Hank returned looking anxious and flushed. He had made certain all the Yards were in the positions where he'd placed them and were on full alert. Their strike force had seventy-six men counting Hank and McManus. This also included two Vietnamese Special Forces sergeants along as observers who acted as if they were on a camping trip and who had already disappeared. Everyone knew they would run away as soon as they could find an exit. Hank and McManus feared their strike force could be outgunned, maybe ten-to-one or even worse when they heard the growing sound of a distant small plane. "They definitely know we're here. Came in too fast to have known earlier. Their trail watcher screwed up, probably off sleeping somewhere. They're trying to figure out our strength," Hank told McManus.

Three Five with his much stronger radio signal and the advantage of higher altitude was briefing Ban Me Thuot as they spoke. McManus estimated, "He'll be here in zero two minutes." Hank nodded, never looking at McManus as he spoke, Hank's wide open eyes constantly moving, laser-like, looking everywhere. "Be back," Hank hissed, hunched low, darting off.

Three Five said visibility improved greatly as he flew towards them. It was now almost ten to one in the afternoon, and he was somewhere overhead. Three Five let out a long low whistle as he said, "Oh God."

"Tell me, tell me," McManus shot back.

"They're on the move. You're circled. They've got a good fix on you, and I see…." his voice trailed off. "I see…, about, two, yeah maybe two battalions…close to maybe a thousand bad guys."

"Roger that," McManus shot back.

"There's something else not too good," Three Five suddenly said.

"What? What? Come on!" McManus said, his voice strained. Three Five gave him the bad news, "I'm almost out of gas. Don't have much time on station." McManus looked up at a flash overhead through the jungle canopy of the little silver plane. Occasional shots rang out, enemy soldiers taking pot shots at the plane.

"I need a big favor?" Three Five said.

"Sure, anything," McManus answered.

"I'll stay till I run dry. You'll need me. If I crash on your orange panel which I can see, get me out of the plane."

McManus looked at his 12 by 12-inch day-glow neon orange signal panel he had spread out on the ground next to his radio. He searched for his friend's plane. He could hear it but not see it, wondering what it would be like to have a plane crash on him. He pictured maybe a thousand North Vietnamese making their run at him. He looked for the little silver plane, didn't see it and vowed, "We'll get you out, Three Five, we'll get you out." Hank listening on the other radio, nodded.

Minutes passed. No gunfire, aside from an occasional shot at the plane. Three Five had white phosphorous rockets on his wings. There were three rockets mounted on the underside of each wing. The rockets were normally smoke canisters for marking enemy position for times when Three Five had air support on station. Three Five had traded the Air Force for some "willy pete" which also marks the position but with a deadly difference. Willy Pete is white phosphorous, burning shards of molten metal that can't be put out with water. If it touches your skin, it burns all the way through.

He offered to mark the largest concentration of the NVA with a rocket. Hank and McManus looked at each other. It would definitely force the issue. The two men lay beside their radios, twenty feet apart, facing opposite directions. They understood what marking the enemy force with willy pete meant. Until this moment, it had been a standoff, both sides moving around, taking stock of the situation, and looking at each other across the misty clearings through the jungle brush. Up in the South Central Highlands, leading Montagnards on combat operations, war was often a game of chess with some jockeying around before a firefight. Sometimes point elements, the lead scouts of two opposing units would talk to each other first, bluffing, delaying the other side before a shot was fired, all the while moving to outflank each other.

McManus looked over at Hank who had listened to everything. Hank gave a shrug like he didn't much care one way or another. He didn't give a rat's ass. He took a big bite out of a piece of NVA fruit. Hank didn't care at all. He'd been here so many times its old stuff. He's so fucking blasé McManus drew strength from Hank's indifference. They're comfortable with whatever comes next. This, the day of his dream, August 17th. McManus was resigned to whatever might happen. He nodded to Hank as Pterodactyl Three Five made a low pass over them. Without hesitating, McManus gave Hank "thumbs up."

Hank smiled, spat out a mouthful of half-chewed fruit. He told Three Five, "Let it happen," speaking into the radio so cool as if he's ordering a pizza.

Rockets swooshed over their heads at downward angles from both wings of the diving plane, exploding not a hundred yards from where they knelt by their radios. They dove flat as white phosphorous burning shards of molten metal ripped through the jungle. No one felt the NVA were that close. Their whole world blew up, seams ripped open, a roar of gunfire sweeping the hill. Waves upon waves of gunfire, smoke, and screams deafened them. McManus knew he'd see Three Five crashing before he'd ever hear him.

For maybe five minutes; grenades, claymore mines, machine guns, AK-47's and carbines on full automatic drowned out their curses and screams. The long antennas are shot off both radios. Hank's radio explodes into smithereens. Parts of the radio dial stick in his arm. Their world is splintering, shit falling down in every direction. The bark, leaves, and branches are flying off McManus' small tree. A confetti shower of minced green covers him completely. Opening his pistol belt, he folds it back on both sides. He ripped open his shirt, even the fly of his pants and peeled them aside, pushing down, crushing himself into the soft mud, getting lower as gunfire crisscrossed the hill. Nowhere to go, no place to hide.

Haze from gunfire and explosions doubled the mist. The air a dirty foam, the roar deafening. McManus couldn't tell if Three Five's plane was still above them, had crashed, or been shot down. He prayed Three Five didn't take him up on his promise at that moment. McManus tried to peek at Hank, now maybe twelve feet away near the shattered pieces of his radio, facing away, looking in the opposite direction. Then he turned toward McManus, mouth roaring curses without sound, shooting his M-16 rifle into the edge of the clearing, empty magazines scattered all around. He turned toward McManus again, his mouth moving, shouting something. McManus couldn't hear a word. Frustrated, Hank turned away, firing methodically at shapes running in the mist.

Deafened, McManus didn't know the firefight had slowed down because he couldn't hear. Hank crawled over to him. McManus stood up, dazed. A bullet zipped by. He didn't flinch, didn't hear it. Hank reached up and pulled him down. McManus' tiger fatigues smeared with mud, his empty canteen ripped by bullets or shrapnel. Hat gone. Hank sat up wrapping a dirty bandage around a bloody gash on his arm. He examined the knot, looked at McManus, pointed to Dolly running their way, then crawled away to check the perimeter.

McManus turned, watching Henry crawl into the mist when a boot kicked him in the side. Dolly is standing over him, livid. McManus had never seen him so angry. Dolly throws his M-16 in the mud in front of McManus. It sticks there, muzzle down, a round jammed in the ejection chamber. They start to draw a lot of fire. Ignoring bullets whipping around, Dolly screams in a mix of Rhade, French, and English. McManus doesn't need an interpreter. He throws his rifle to Dolly who takes it, turns to run back to where he had been fighting, then stops as if snagged on something.

Over his shoulder, Dolly looks curiously at him. McManus could see his mind working. Dolly knows McManus doesn't have another weapon. His face softens, he mouths, "Merci." It's a weird moment that doesn't belong, doesn't fit any script. A feeling between two men frozen in a death-dancing-strobe of chaotic emotion, something beyond expression. The firefight intensifies dramatically. Looking at the useless weapon stuck in the mud, McManus gives Dolly *the finger*. Laughing, Dolly runs away with the rifle.

Crouched low with Dolly's broken rifle, he hustles back to the command post near the one good radio just as an explosion rocks the area. A concussion coming from trees above throws him to the ground. He thought it was Pterodactyl Three Five crashing on him and rolled over looking up. It wasn't Three Five but a lot of jungle canopy coming down. He kept rolling, burying his face in the mud, lacing his hands over the back of his head.

Shrapnel whistled through the underbrush as branches, leaves, and debris bury him, the weight pushing him into the mud. Been about two minutes since he'd seen Dolly. The last explosion was probably an NVA mortar round. Buried in the fallen tree, he lay there reaching for Dolly's rifle. Can't be fixed. Useless! What the hell? McManus crawled over to the radio. He switched the antennas, replacing the damaged long one for a short flexible antenna. Testing it, McManus still couldn't hear well. Impossible to communicate except through hand signals. He could hear something, the NVA blowing their shrill policeman-like whistles to direct and control their attack. He wondered if Three Five was up there somewhere or burning in the jungle.

He hadn't noticed any fly-overs in a long time. Would Three Five come crashing in on them unannounced? If Three Five tried to warn him by radio, he might not hear it. He hoped he'd see him in time to get out of the way. McManus thought about getting killed by a plane hitting him in the middle of the jungle in a lopsided firefight. Fate scoring a cosmic bull's eye. He smiled at this, then saw Hank looking at him again.

They huddle and sent out a radio transmission, Hank seems to have better hearing, but his voice is raw. McManus can't hear well, but his voice is okay. The transmission goes out in the "blind" not knowing who'd hear them. The message: "Any station this is Bat Guano. Surrounded, low on ammunition. Send

anything, *Prairie Fire! Prairie Fire!* Negative further. Out."
Prairie Fire a term used *only* when a unit's being overrun.

Legs weak, McManus sat down leaning against the small tree. He is at ease with himself and the moment. He feels composed as he slumps back against what is left of the little tree near his radio. He settles himself as if in a chair on the beach and lets out a long slow breath, taking stock of their situation. Surrounded, outnumbered possibly by twenty to one according to Three Five's overhead estimate. They have no artillery or air support, no medivac, resupply or reinforcements. He has a survival knife and a few smoke grenades within arm's reach. In his mind's eye, he plays back the image of the small Montagnard giggling as he looked back at McManus before disappearing in the mist that morning, mimicking McManus' words *Many Beaucoup Magics.* McManus laughs again. He can't hear himself laughing but sees Hank looking at him.

Hank hasn't stopped shaking his head angrily every time he looks at McManus since he saw him give Dolly his rifle. He reads Hank's lips, "You're bug-fuck nuts." Hank's seen at lot; now he's seen it all. He keeps looking at McManus, shaking his head. McManus doesn't care. He has been living some variation of this moment for a long time. The firefight over for a moment. It's only been maybe twenty minutes since Three Five fired those rockets and disappeared from the sky. He hoped Three Five was okay somewhere. If he'd crashed, no one would know where.

This is the eye of the storm, each side adjusting for another run at the other. For the Strike Force there wouldn't be any running;

nowhere to go. Hank knew from Dolly and Whet that his Yards were where they should be and, miraculously, no one had been hurt. The little ammunition they had been redistributed. In the eerie silence, there were no sounds or signals they could hear. No detectable enemy movement, voices, or whistles. There didn't seem to be any reason for this. The throbbing hellish pounding in the ears after a firefight is an unimaginable sensation. The eyes burn, throats rasp in pain from screaming to be heard.

McManus spat blood. Smoke from explosions, gunfire clouded the mist. McManus noted it wasn't the mist from his dreams, not a mist of many colors. Picking up the radio, he tried to raise Pterodactyl Three Five. If he pressed the handset microphone into his ear, he could barely hear a little. At least he could hear himself again.

Suddenly he hears Three Five's voice. They're both excited to hear each other had survived and kept interrupting one another, amazed they're both alive, unhurt. Three Five starts to tell McManus incredible things are going down. McManus says he doesn't have to be told the circus is in town, he and Hank are in the middle ring. Three Five tells them they've got to hold on a few more minutes. McManus is laughing. Hank's frowning. The only sound is the plane somewhere up in the thick white stuff and McManus' voice on the radio talking to it. Hank looks as if he'd like to shoot him.

Three Five is animated, "No, no, listen up! Hueys, not gunships but slicks with M-60 door gunners, stranded west of the storm days ago." Three Five didn't go into it, but the helicopters had gotten trapped behind the storm front several days earlier and sat three days at an A-team on the border somewhere north of Tieu Atar. When the weather started to break they were up in the air, trying to work their way around the northern edge of the storm toward Pleiku. Once they were up, they heard McManus' Strike Force was about to be over-run, so they diverted, taking a dead run due south. Three Five, ecstatic with this good luck, hollers "Five, ten minutes out, these guys can sting!"

Hank asks to have a Huey swing by Tieu Atar and pick up some ammo. Wasn't sure his Yards had much sting left. Three Five in a supercritical fuel situation said he'd leave soon as he had the choppers "visual." Could see McManus' neon orange day glow panel lying on the ground and said he'd aim for it if he stalled. McManus promised again he'd get Three Five out of the plane if it crashed. "Gotta land on us man; can't be making house calls."

"Forever" ticked off on McManus' watch. He listened. Thought he could hear the distant "whumping" sound of inbound helicopters. Three Five said he could see them and was heading back to Tieu Atar. McManus heard the sound of the flight leader calling him.

"Bat Guano, Bat Guano, this is Stagecoach Two Zero, over."

"Stagecoach this is Bat Guano. Read you five-by. I'll mark with smoke, over."

The Colors, the Noise and the Mist

McManus gestured to Hank for smoke grenades. He tossed two over to McManus who had two of his own. He didn't know if he could get all four out to mark their irregular perimeter in time. He took off on the run across the hill where the heaviest fighting had been, looking for Montagnards. In a low crouch, he ran forty, fifty yards. An AK-47 fired at McManus, splintering a nearby thicket of bamboo. He popped smoke throwing the billowing grenade over the heads of three Montagnards crouched in a hole filled with water.

He ran back up the hill in another direction. The gunfire had stopped. He ran past more Yards crouched in another small foxhole. One of them was the little Yard who had the dream about today. The little dreamer's face was an incredulous study of amazement as he watched McManus run past him throwing a bright red smoke grenade. The Yard cringed as gunfire started up again. McManus yelled "Yo! Many beaucoup magics!" turning sharply, gunfire wracking nearby bamboo. McManus got off another grenade as soon as he located more Yards on the outer perimeter.

Moving fast, running through the mists, McManus feared breaking through the narrow line separating his guys from the enemy. He ran behind two men lying in the wrong direction. They weren't Yards, they were NVA. Turning to get a shot, they forced McManus to change direction again. Slipping, he fell, dropping his last grenade. Speed crawling to it, he took off running, pin out of the grenade, curls of billowing purple smoke trailing. One last grenade, burning his hand, thick smoke dying his arm and hand purple, had to get rid of it, but not yet. As he ran past Hank at the radio, halfway down the front of the hill. McManus threw his last grenade as far as he could in the direction Dolly had run off with his rifle. Back up the hill again he slid head-first across the clearing to the radio, Hank shooting full automatic barely over McManus' head.

The North Vietnamese start screaming, ramping up for what McManus had heard of but never experienced, a human wave assault. A loud eerie sound came from all sides at once as the enemy stoked themselves to charge into the smoke. A sound louder and eerier than anything McManus had ever heard. Like a shrill cheer from wailing souls, with no choice but to come forward, the sound morbid, darkly hysterical, death about to make its visit, opening a door into eternity, long shadows darkening the mist. McManus struck dumb by the sound of his dream.

Two-Zero's voice comes out of the radio right on top of them, about to light-up everything outside the smoke. Smoke from McManus' grenades moving in thick, brilliant ribbons of color interwoven across the hill, mixing through the mist. The NVA momentarily silent, knowing helicopters are going to open up on everything outside the ring of smoke. McManus looks at his purple hand, laughing. He doesn't feel the burns. Hank is beating his fist in the mud. He gives in. Hank starts laughing.

Stagecoach hollering out of the handset, "Bat Guano, I see purple, yellow and red smoke. Which one are you?" McManus looks at the thick vivid colors mixing over him. Christ, he'd unleashed three different colors with his four grenades. Two deep purples, a school bus yellow, a rich lipstick red. It's all there, the colors, the noise, and the mist. He hears the North Vietnamese start another loud hysterical human wave scream. Somewhere in the jungle, their leader is putting a whistle in his mouth about to blow the signal, a blast from hell, sending them running banzai nuts into McManus' little ring. McManus screams into the radio: "That's all us! Shoot it! Shoot now! Now!" A laughing Hank hollers "Many Beaucoup Magics." Explosions of gunfire swallow their words.

The North Vietnamese come out of the jungle in screaming human waves. Five helicopters bank "danger close" right on top of McManus' small perimeter in an ever-tightening circle, safety no consideration. Known as a "daisy chain," the equivalent of five cars bumper to bumper running at ninety miles an hour only a few car lengths between them. All this banked steeply at tree-top level, taking heavy automatic weapons fire from below. Situation left Stagecoach Two-Zero and his crew no option. Their 25-foot rotor blades clipped treetops, a shower of leafy confetti floating down from their macabre merry-go-round. An incredible roar from ten machine guns firing 6000 rounds per minute shredding the jungle. Man-made lightning splaying everywhere. Blinding flashes, bullets ricocheting off bullets. Thousands of red tracer bullets per minute arced down on the small strike force huddled in the mystical circle of McManus' swirling colors of smoke. Ninety-mile-an-hour winds from the five choppers in the trees creating a gale force mixing the colors against a background of gray drizzle. Concentrations of tracer bullets so intense they resemble glowing red neon tubes of light lacing the air. North Vietnamese everywhere, a surrealistic miasma, death and madness, the little perimeter collapsing in on itself. Like the children's game King of the Mountain, only those who make it inside the whirling dervish of color will live.

McManus takes a boot in the ribs, Dolly standing over him, kicking, screaming, pointing at the sky. McManus looks up at gunships firing down on their perimeter! Everywhere door gunners firing straight at them. Couldn't hear Dolly, but got the message. Bullets kicking up mud, shredding bamboo and trees, dinging off the radios and anything lying about. McManus tackles Dolly to protect him as gunships roar ever lower, louder. Two men wrestling in the mud. Machine gun fire rips into everything.

In the light gray drizzle, flashing light from tracers casts the fight in lazy freeze-frames. No one could move without getting blasted. Covered in mud, Dolly wriggles out of his grasp, McManus screaming he can't stop it. No one could hear him, not even Dolly, inches away. He runs away with McManus' rifle.

McManus becomes strangely detached. An awareness of mist, light, color, and sound so great it seems to come from inside. Everything crawls in slow motion. Feeling fascination with what must be the end of his life, his prophesized end, McManus knows his dream has come to life and now to death. Maybe ten more seconds to live. Ten seconds! A lifetime, down to the last few heartbeats. It's over. Nothing can change his fate.

An epiphany, his test had been that rifle!

Dice rolled.

Game played.

Dice to rest.

However it ends, he's done all he can. It's all right, it's what it is, it's all it can be.

Overwhelming roar obliterates all sound.

Noise draws sound into a vacuum.

He hears nothing.

All the sound and energy of the day explodes into silence.

One last thought as he loses consciousness: "Is *this* what death is?"

To the Same God

Lying on his back, McManus looked up at a canopy now bare of leaves, at an empty blue sky. The storm lifted. The sun has come out. A blanket of chopped green leaves and little branches a foot thick covers him.

Hank and Whet stand looking down at him. He looks like a head sticking out of a salad. They're grinning. He looks up at them, smiles warily as if seeing an apparition. A halo of sunlight surrounds them. All of them filthy, exhausted, drained of energy. Their clothes are in tatters. McManus sits up, twigs and leaves falling out of his hair. The only sound, helicopters muted and far away, fading to a soft flutter, then dying out.

Hank's mouth moves. He is saying something. McManus can make out some words. Others come to him from lip reading. Little by little he can follow Hank's thoughts. He says the enemy had just gotten to the perimeter when the gunships opened up. A very large soldier leading the charge fell within twelve feet of McManus. The man certainly hadn't been there when he was mud-wrestling with Dolly. An officer, the man has a Russian automatic pistol near his hand. Hank thinks he might be Chinese. Never know for sure. The NVA's front lines just entered the circle of smoke when the ring of helicopters literally built a solid wall of lead, both door gunners on each chopper firing their M-60's from one side, absolute devastation. McManus thinks of his Yards. He feels sick, "Oh shit!"

Hank spoke. "Where'd you come up with 'Many beaucoup magics'?" McManus looked at him. He can hear him. "Not one of us came off with so much as a scratch!" He watches McManus closely, waiting. All this sinking in.

The moment broken as a helicopter drops down, hovering in the trees, bringing another green shower of shredded leaves. A hasty warning "duck," comes out of the radio a little too late. "Duck" the last word that radio ever communicates. Crates of ammunition, grenades, even a case of warm beer from 40 feet up cascade down on the radio next to the neon day-glow marker panel. Bad place to leave your only radio. A perfect bulls-eye. Hank, McManus, and Whet scramble for their lives. A waterfall of wooden crates continues to fall from the sky. Heavy cases of C-rations and grenades crushing their only workable radio, destroying it, cutting off someone's voice mid-message.

McManus and Hank limp around the hill surveying the damage, reassuring the Yards, consolidating their position, preparing to spend the night. An hour before dusk a relief column reaches them, led by Tyre, the team medic who shouldn't have left camp. He was exhausted, having run cross-country over thirteen kilometers through the sometimes dense jungle. Tyre's hands, neck, and face are flushed and bloody from fighting his way through razor sharp elephant grass for over four hours. He missed the battle but he came, courageously foolish, running full speed to the sound of the fight, to his friends and teammates outnumbered, surrounded and about to be overrun.

Tyre's a hero in the purest sense of the word. His only reward how McManus and Hank respect him. Hell, they loved him! Tyre showed up so far in front of his Montagnards some straggled in for an hour. Hank kept smiling, saying "And the sweet mother fucker did it with a radio heavier than a case of beer on his back. A radio, a fucking beautiful radio!" Russ Tyre, the man who had chopped down the tree that crushed their last truck: Hero of the Day. Tyre kept staring at McManus and Hank incredulously, saying he couldn't believe how dirty they were. He loved how McManus' hand and arm had gotten dyed purple from running with that last hot smoke grenade. He kept looking at him laughing. "You look really fucking weird Sir." Good to have company. Great to have Tyre and his men with you as the shadows grew longer in the afternoon light. And a radio to boot.

Whet reported not one casualty of any kind in their strike force. Hank is saying something to McManus when Dolly walks up with a slight limp, grinning. McManus' mind keeps wandering. He can't believe there are no friendly casualties. Hank and Whet reassure him. The enemy lost a lot of men, at least thirty-some, certainly many more, scattered all over the area. Hank gestured towards Dolly's leg, the limp. Dolly waved him off. In flawless

French, he says "Pas de quoi," *it is nothing*, as he lights his cigarette, imitating Bogart convincingly. He'd learned the expression from Bat Guano who learned it from Rozanski, a WW II Polish hero. They all laugh and slip back into the movie of their lives.

A search of the larger area turned up an enormous cache of rice and weapons on the far side of the enemy base camp. It was impossible to know if the enemy had been bringing in more supplies or stopping to pick them up, but McManus knew it was a key to their disastrous hesitation. The enemy should have pressed a fast attack, but didn't. That made all the difference. Once the choppers showed up, everything changed forever. McManus and Hank realize they'd never know what made the NVA hesitate. When they started that fight, there was no way anyone could have known helicopters would be in the air behind the storm front, capable of getting to them. The enemy must have thought they had time to secure their treasure of supplies, then attack. Somebody screwed up. So many things reeling through McManus' mind.

Such a strange day; such a peculiar war. McManus wonders if this is all "A dream within a dream?"

"What the fuck was *That* all about?" McManus says to no one in particular.

Pterodactyl Three Five had headed back to the little airfield at Tieu Atar once Stagecoach acknowledged he had a fix on McManus' position, the little plane coasted in on fumes, barely making the end of the runway. Hank and Tyre had patrols finding blood trails, bodies, and equipment everywhere, but not one Montagnard had so much as a scratch. Unbelievable! Hank kept saying, "Many beaucoup magics," and laughing hysterically. He looked at McManus, taking the measure of him and said very seriously, "You're a stone crazy fool, give Dolly your rifle, an' go off running around the green fucking jungle with nothing but fucking smoke grenades!" He'd work himself up, get angry, laugh, shake his head. "What's the use? What's the fuckin' use?" He kept describing McManus scrambling up the hill, "Out of the fucking mist, gunfire splintering bamboo all around you, looking like a big goofy grape coming at me dyed in thick purple smoke. You pulled the pin early! Why'd you pull the pin? You're as crazy as you are lucky. Lucky I didn't shoot you!" He'd laugh himself into spasms, shake his head, and repeat the whole story again. Hank was happy to be alive, drained, exhausted, but happy to be alive. Their warm beer tasted great.

The Montagnards had their own mystical take on what happened. They squatted in a circle, talking it over. To a man, they agreed everything tied into McManus' dream, what he'd told the Yards that morning in response to the dream they'd brought him. McManus had been handed a great test. The "Old Ones" had spoken through dreams to prepare McManus, to protect them. Whet said emphatically that McManus giving his rifle to Dolly changed everything. Might have turned out much differently, much worse for all of them. Whet was certain, he wouldn't give any ground on this. Something singularly unique had occurred. The Spirits were pleased. McManus wasn't comfortable about this but kept quiet.

He didn't know what he *knew* anymore.

Hank, Cheshire-cat grin on his face, mimicked him, having a beer and a good time as if even he accepted that giving up your gun could change everything. McManus had gotten an "A+" on his big test.

Dolly, either distracted or overcome, had little to say. Voice strained, he kept spitting blood. He'd bitten his tongue. He gave McManus a muddy bear hug, took off one of his Montagnard bracelets and put it on McManus' wrist. It was a great honor. No words for this moment. The feeling that accompanied the bracelet came from how Dolly looked at McManus. Something of battle and brotherhood overwhelmed them. The two men couldn't speak.

Dolly offered to return the M-16. McManus told him he didn't need it. Said he could defend himself with color and smoke. They started laughing again. Another case of beer with more ammunition, another radio, even an M-16 for McManus arrived. This time, lowered through the canopy. There was even a "church key" for the beer. McManus handed beers to Whet and Dolly. Hot beers, geysering out when popped open, spraying Whet and Hank, missing McManus. Hank danced out of the way, a little too late, laughing, "Even beer can't hit Bat Guano." The men drank a toast to life, to their life. Ten feet away lay an enemy soldier who would dream no more. Or maybe now he would dream forever.

McManus put down his beer, walking away from the group to stand over the man who had been killed. A light rain fell. Exhausted, McManus had nothing left to give. The mist lifted, occasional sun above the canopy, a lingering pastel smoke-bomb color moving in mingled streams, a miasma of vague color slowly crisscrossing the hill. If anything the air had a slight pink tinge to it. In the strange light, McManus bent down and opened the man's shirt revealing a corroded religious medal and whistle. The man had been Catholic. McManus was Catholic and wore the Saint Christopher medal his Mother gave him. Touching his neck, he felt his Mother's keepsake next to his dog tags.

Two Mothers praying in different languages to the same God to bring their sons home unharmed.

Two sons, wearing almost identical religious medals, trying to kill one another.

He stood up and tried to say a prayer.

It wouldn't come to him.

When he first got to this war, he had trouble getting his hands on a weapon. This day of his dream he had given his weapon away.

McManus took a poncho, covering the man, then went off by himself to sit down under the tattered war-torn tree where his radio had been earlier.

He began absentmindedly heating water in his dented little green C-ration can. Just something to do. Like the busy-work that goes on when there's death in a family. There's a poem by Emily Dickinson about this, but he couldn't remember it clearly. The thought of it was just there with him, undefined like the mist that softened in the parting daylight. Sitting under a tree almost bare of its bark, leaves, and branches, McManus felt a change coming over him, a profound sense he'd better make sense of all this. Something inside of him wasn't right. Something amiss in his soul, deep inside him where his "meanings" were. He'd done everything expected of him. He'd served his country and stepped up when needed. He'd kept the promise he'd made as a little boy. All he ever wanted to do was "the right thing." He wasn't comfortable with where all this had taken him.

When it came time to walk off this little hill, McManus knew he'd never be the same. Many men paid big on this day. He wasn't one of them. He had skated free. Somehow he knew he'd survived yet hadn't won, not in the sense he'd always understood "winning." When death on such a grand scale becomes as much of his life as it had this day, he realized winning and losing can't be weighed on the same scales as living and dying.

A Hushed Requiem

In the fading late afternoon light, McManus remembered a little boy hiding in the shadows, eavesdropping on his uncles telling stories about their war.

Johnny felt at peace for the very first time about his father not going to war. He knew he'd never be able to tell his uncles about August 17th in any way they'd understand. Some things can't be put into words.

He never finished making coffee. The water boiled, the fire flickered, his flame died. The water sat untouched, cooling, fading like the light.

Hank, Tyre, and the Montagnards left him alone, moving away to speak in whispers. He sat looking at the man covered by a poncho, the afternoon fading, pink mist to dusk, then inky darkness. The jungle was unusually quiet; the wildlife driven away by the afternoon's violence. He sat in a hush. The little hill made sacred by everything that happened here. This night a wake for a man who had been his enemy.

Johnny McManus curled up and fell asleep saying a prayer for this Vietnamese soldier's Mother who would suffer all her days wondering what happened to her child.

"The worst wasn't to die, but to see one's soul change."

Father Jeandel, French Paratroop Chaplain,
French Indo-China War

Southern Wind

Long home from that journey
Here with Penelope happily at her loom
The color of last night still lovely in our cheeks
All is peace.
Yet in me there cries this restless voice
And though I somehow know better
That part of me where my *meanings* are
Paces in the past, there only do I live.
To stand again on wooden, cold, high-winded decks
Facing the north-west ice rains
Those sleeted tears from home
So alive, all that storied night
Pursuing the darkness, always full sail.
In sleep, I also dream of other times
And in that composed slice of death
I dream of thunder red battle days
Achilles at my side
Our strong slashing bloodied arms
Swinging fabled and great weighted swords
Back to back we denied the world
Access to our vulnerabilities.
Later, by the fire, on the reddened sands
Tasting the wood-casqued home wine
Mourning those whose lives have splintered
I find I look with longing to the distant sea

And in my dream of war, I dream of home.   Tom Garvey

Tom Garvey

Acknowledgments

Many Beaucoup Magics is a true story. It comes from a promise made to the Mothers of seven friends lost in the war. In various ways, I became close to these Mothers and sent cards or called them over the years keeping in touch. I bear an obligation to tell a story that neither glorifies nor romanticizes war. To their last breath, they never got over the loss of their children, to me, they represent the ultimate victims of war.

I am grateful to Bob Shryock, our Three Five, for all he ever did for me and the men who lived on the border. He was a friend and a hero to us. Respect tinged with awe abides for all those who came to our aid when we needed them.

I am also grateful to Al Owen, Stagecoach Two Zero, and his crew chief Monk Andrews for the complete disregard for their own safety on the most poignant and harrowing day of my life. These men and those who flew with them saved our lives. They were incredible. "Clear left," Monk.

One member of Stagecoach Two-Zero's crew deserves special mention. His name is Armando Ramirez, and he was the other door gunner with Monk Andrews. Armando never came home from Vietnam and is still listed as missing in action from an extremely dangerous mission on the 23rd of May, 1969. His helicopter went down in Cambodia. Armando was just twenty years old at the time and had extended his tour in Vietnam. My deepest respect and gratitude go out to his family in Wilcox, Arizona for their sacrifice and our loss. Please Remember Armando Ramirez and those who loved him in your most profound moments.

Armando Ramirez, 155th AHC, Ban Me Thuot

February 01, 1949-May 23, 1969

Tour of Duty: March 15, 1968-May 23,1969

To the best of my knowledge the man, I referred to as Vernon K Sutton did not lose his leg and returned home after an honorable tour as did the lieutenant captured at the outpost near Ben Het. He endured many years as a prisoner of war and returned home with honor.

I don't know if this story will ever find its way to Bill Murray but when I saw him singing The Ballad of the Green Berets in Caddyshack I got a kick out of it and wondered if he ever imagined that one of his cousins, the grandson of Kitty Sheehan from Chicago, ran around on the Cambodian Border with a bunch of Montagnards who thought his name was Bat Guano.

I am grateful for all of the courageous and competent good men who served with me and my wish for them is that they live long and well and are surrounded all their days by those who love and understand them.

A very special thank you to Hugh Gilmore, Elizabeth Burchard, Roy Hughes, Donald Ulysses Smith, and Lloyd Kern as well as Larry Woodlock, Special Forces Medic, known as "The Ghost of Dak Seang," A-245, for their relentless proofreading and advice. Thank you to Kathy at The Muse House Center for the Literary Arts in Philadelphia for support and encouragement. Thank you to Annie Hart, my little Neuro-linguistic Programmer for guiding me back to the path so I could complete a story I have worked on for almost fifty years and well over 10,000 hours.

The old Vietnamese man sitting on the ground, holding a string tied to his scrawny, gimpy chicken haunts me to this day as does the fate of our sweet and innocent Montagnards who really did love us "beaucoup too much."

Frederick W. Henry retired from the Army as a Sergeant Major and lived in Wallingford, Connecticut where he passed away on February 12th, 2015. Hank was loved and respected by his five daughters as well as his companion, Lorri, a high school sweetheart. Knowing he had these women in his life gives me peace when I think of Hank who remains the finest Special Forces Team Sergeant and most courageous soldier I've ever known. It is an honor to have served with him. I will miss him all my days.

And last, but most important, Many Beaucoup Magics exists solely because of the never faltering love, belief, and support of my best friend, Peggy Garvey. She is also my wife and sweetheart. I am in awe of her every day, and that life brought her gifts to me. My greatest joy and reward is that I may live all my days with her and will be able to always love her "too much."

Fini, Het Roi

Tom Garvey / once aka "bat guano"

Ambler, Pennsylvania   19002

Tgarvey702@aol.com

About the Author

Tom Garvey, an Airborne, Ranger, and Special Forces officer served as an A-Team Leader in Vietnam in 1968 and returned home in late January 1969, to mixed reviews about his stability and state of mind. Like many other Vietnam Veterans, he found few cared to hear about his time overseas. Within one week of his homecoming, he was a full-time college student during the day and working from midnight to eight a.m., six days a week, in the *Blade Shop* at Westinghouse, Lester, Pennsylvania. In 1971 he graduated *Magna Cum Laude* from Widener University in Chester, Pennsylvania. After college, the kindest way to put it is that "the wheels came off" and he managed with menial jobs until he met his future wife, Peggy. She is the best thing that ever happened to him. From the day they met in July 1983, Tom felt he had finally come home. He married for the first time at the age of fifty and is blessed with a wonderful family of five stepchildren and their mates and two world-class granddaughters. Life is good. Life is very good indeed. He has come home.

"And in my dream of war, I dream of home."

Made in the USA
Middletown, DE
19 February 2019